WHERE DO I GO FROM HERE?

Where Do I Go from Here?

Published by Gatekeeper Press
2167 Stringtown Rd, Suite 109
Columbus, OH 43123-2989
www.GatekeeperPress.com

Library of Congress Control Number: 2020949187

ISBN (hardcover): 9781662906138
eISBN: 9781662906145

WHERE DO I GO FROM HERE?

A Memoir

Torrey C. Butler

gatekeeper press
Where Authors are Family ™
Columbus, Ohio

Being me is easy. Becoming me wasn't.

CONTENTS

WHERE DO I GO FROM HERE?

Noun: this title describes a person, place, thing, or idea.

You probably never paid it much thought, but this question is asked a lot. Whether you ask aloud or question from within, this may sometimes be the hardest question to answer. Whether you are asking for directions or trying to navigate through this tough world we live in, where do you go? The title *Where Do I Go from Here* addresses your ongoing search for direction, relationships, a fresh start, advice, guidance, acceptance, love, *true happiness*, internal joy, financial stability, stability, elevation, lust, control, *peace*, peace of mind, *forgiveness*, compassion, laughter, conversation, revenge, companionship, pity, structure, comprehension, options, permanent people, permanent situations, redos, growth, understanding, luck, blessings, humanity, belonging, kindness, laughter, support, company, a shoulder to cry on, *substance*, motivation, *freedom*, independence, patience, life, individuality, sex, style, *counseling*, assistance, guidance, equality, equity, payment, *God*, consistency, strength, improvement, success, durability, camaraderie, friendship, relief, personality, affection, loyalty, time, faithfulness, mercy, trust, partnership, *purpose*, a way out, favor, support, accomplishments, an escape, justice, warmth, wisdom, education, opportunity, free will, *you*—as long as you live on this earth, you will always be in search of something that is meaningful to you.

I'm still in search of things myself, some of them emphasized with italics so you can see that I'm not perfect, nor do I have it all together. I am human, perfectly imperfect just like you. The strange part is just because you find what you're searching for doesn't mean you'll have it forever. The search for everything mentioned is always ongoing, depending on what season of life you find yourself in. In one stage of life, you could be searching for peace and forgiveness. But in another stage in your life, you could be searching for revenge and payback but also understanding. It all *just* depends.

We are all going through this amusement park called life, figuring out rides we like, which ones make us sick, and which thrills bring us happiness. But one thing that remains true, regardless of our current situations, is that we will always ask ourselves, "Where do I go from here?" This question can only be answered by one individual, the one person who is in control of the life you live, the person reading this right now. Stay tuned for my ride.

POEM

Started: December 10, 2019   Completed: December 29, 2019

Time: 7:43 a.m. PST   Time: 1:27 a.m. PST

Let Me Catch You Up on Life
A Poem by Torrey C. Butler

Sheesh. I'm twenty-five now.

Do you know the percentage of young black kids that grow up without fathers and still make something of themselves?

It's twenty-five now.

You *see*, there is soooo much that happened in my life.

Well, wait, I guess that's the point: you didn't *see* it, so please let me catch you up on life.

December of '93 a king was born, and I know you were so ecstatic, so elated, probably acting so dramatic.

I could imagine you bragging to your boys in the hospital room that day saying, "Yeahh, my son is here! And I can't wait for y'all to meet him!"

I could say the same. I couldn't wait to meet you either.

But it's a shame that you didn't show up; it's a shame you never came.

I tried to come up with every excuse for you.

Where were you? Don't worry; I'll wait for an answer.

Nah, fuck that. I waited long enough, twenty-five years to be exact, hoping that I could understand what and where you lacked, hoping you would pick up the pieces to try and win me and Mom back…but.

Maybe that's just the good idea fairy talking.

But enough about you, this is about me. You *see*, because there is soooo much that happened in my life.

Well, wait. I guess that's the point: you didn't *see* it, so please let me catch you up on life.

I can go on and on about the "wasn'ts," but I'd rather address what was.

I graduated high school. I earned a full-ride scholarship to college. I graduated magna cum laude from Savannah State University. I'm a Black commissioned officer in the United States Navy. And my biggest blessing, I am having a beautiful baby girl.

Oh yeah, Dad, and…Nah, me filling you in stops here.

My daughter will read this poem one day and have no idea what all this means.

She will never have to catch me up on her life, I'll be too busy being caught all in it.

BEFORE I GET STARTED...

More than three years later, I *finally* finished this memoir. I remember how the idea came up too. I was in college, or even before that, I was in high school. I had a lot of things happen around me during that time, some positive and some negative, but it took a calm approach to make it through. With everything going on around me, someone said that they could see a movie being made about me, very jokingly. And, of course, I laughed it off right there with them and moved on. Fast-forward to my senior year of college, I was doing the most random thing. I think that's how ideas normally hit people anyway, during spontaneous moments that have nothing to do with anything. I was riding my Gold bike down to the Student Union, also known as the U, to get some food from the Chicken Shack.

On my bike ride there, I was listening to music when the thought popped into my head. It hit me so hard that I could've fallen off my bike. "Remember that movie thing you joked about in high school? Write a book about it. Write a book about your life. Someone needs to see it."

In my mind and heart, I believed that this could actually be something I was supposed to do, but, of course, I needed the validation of other people. I went to a friend of mine and mentioned the idea to him. I'll never forget his response. He smirked and laughed in my face. Not gonna flex, it hurt my feelings because I valued his opinion. I believe in signs. The idea of telling my life story coming up in high school wasn't by mistake, and for it to reappear four years later was no coincidence. I valued other people's opinions heavily at the time, so for him to laugh at me, at me putting my life on the line, hurt, but I think that was exactly what I needed. That was the motivation I needed that flipped the switch. So on July 16, 2017, at 5:05 p.m. PST, I made my first entry. I decided to write what was in my heart and not give a fuck who wasn't fuckin' with it.

More than three years later to this publishing date, I mark this memoir complete. Well, it's not really complete because it's about my life, but you get the point. I know the golden question is why did it take three plus years for me to finish? Honestly, it's like any other project. You want to make sure you capture the right moments, the right angles, and use the *write* words—get it? The "write" words. Anyway, I demanded perfection from myself, and I wanted to make sure the work I put out into the world said what I wanted it to say. I'm thinking legacy-type work. When I am long gone, I'd have a product to tell a quick story about me.

At the same time, those three plus years weren't just filled with writing. They were filled with excitement at times, doubt most of the time, and flat-out I-just-need-to-stop-right-here-because-no-one-is-going-to-read-this thoughts. What I am getting at is I talked myself out of doing this the majority of those years. But that's how dreams normally start, and that's how they normally end.

I learned quickly that I was my biggest motivator, but at times, I could also be my biggest hindrance. The best advice I can offer for that is when you feel yourself doubting yourself, think about this. Number one—it's natural, and it's OK. But once you feel that doubt and hesitation setting in, realize it's happening and smile at it. Then get back to work. My biggest motivation though to keep going was this. I'm looking for that one soul, that one heart who reads this during the many hardships life brings, and it change their minds. Brings them hope. That's my why. Not for book sales, not to become the most readable writer (if that's even a thing), no accolades. This book is going to get me and you through.

AS REAL AS IT GETS

Damn! Why me? Sometimes I wonder if I was born at the right time, at the right second. With all of the bad times and bad news life brings, it gets hard, almost unbearable, to truly believe that you can make it. As I ponder my life, I wonder why I had to endure certain obstacles that seemed to miss everyone else. Man, I swear, it seemed like I was the only person going through shit.

While everyone else was smiling, I was frowning inside. When everyone would come to school in the newest and most expensive brands of clothes, flexing how much their parents cared about their wardrobe, I was wearing the same jeans four days straight hoping no one would call me out. But going through life, you find out who your true friends are. The fake friends will disguise themselves as the real thing, and it can be hard to tell the difference at first. But once you fully examine it, you see the flaws that weren't so apparent before. I found out that the people you think have your back through the rough times really don't. Because of the great person I am, kind and genuine with my actions, people usually take my friendship for granted. I figured out that I cannot put myself in predicaments to be there for others when they don't want to be there for themselves.

Put yourself in this story, this journey. Yeah, this was written about me, but this is also about you. If you ever had to cry yourself to sleep, this story is about you. If you have ever been doubted and deemed a failure by people who did not believe in you, this story is about you. I was never verbally told that I wouldn't be anything growing up, but people's actions showed me that they believed it. If you ever had to sleep in cars because you had no home to lay your head and you looked over to your Mom shivering because she wrapped you in the only blanket she had to stay warm, this story is about you. If you have a story to tell, this is about you. With each sentence that includes the words *me*, *my*, or *I*, think of yourself and the struggles you have endured. Think about the struggles that you are going through now.

Never give up on your dreams despite how hard it gets. And believe me, it will get hard. You will get so many doors slammed in your face, so many dirty looks from people thinking to themselves that you don't belong. When that happens, when that moment happens, remind yourself of who you are and then show them. Believe in the process that God is going to bring you through.

My story needs to be heard. Your story needs to be heard. Our story needs to be heard. Each and every one of us has undergone trials and measures that tested us—trials and measures that we thought at one point we were not going to make it through. Oh yeah, the amount of doubt you placed on your shoulders to talk yourself out of what is for you!

The truth of the matter is the struggles only make us stronger—stronger mentally. I had enough turning points in my life where I wanted to throw in the towel, plenty of times when I did not want to fight on anymore. I wanted to use everything that was negatively happening around me as an excuse not to make something positive of myself—from being homeless and being raised by a single mom to experiencing death firsthand and a system telling me I wasn't smart enough to excel in education. Instead of using those negatives and believing them, I decided to believe something insane and ridiculous. I decided to believe that I could.

Even writing this book, there were times when I wanted to stop and hit backspace delete on every word. I kept thinking to myself, *This is a corny idea.* I thought to myself that I was way out of my element and was shooting a little too high. *Who is going to listen to me? Nobody is going to read this, so I am just wasting my time.*

Right there, I was talking myself out of my own goal. Most of the time, we make it easier for other people to control our lives because we talk ourselves out of the dreams we have. I am done proving other people right that I can't do something. I'd rather show that I can. I had to dig deep and continue to remind myself that there is someone, somewhere who needs to see and hear through the struggles of a kid who endured the same things and can relate. That is what this book is about: believing in yourself when no one else does.

When fifty eyes are looking down on you, your two eyes are looking up, as you know that you can accomplish the unthinkable. I used what can be called my downfalls and hard times as motivation to write this. Our stories need to be heard. Your story needs to be heard. Forget a critic, forget a hater, because they are always gonna have something to say. Right or wrong, true or false.

As you go through the bits and pieces of my life in this writing, don't forget to make it personal to you. We all have something we can learn from each other's setbacks, and I hope that mine can help you get through yours. Your story matters. Make them remember that you were here and that you had a positive impact on this world. This is my story, raw and authentic.

CHAPTER 1
CRAWL BEFORE YOU WALK

If I could repeat this life, I wouldn't change a thing. It's kind of funny; we go through life and wish we could've done things better, differently, all the time. But changing how you do something changes the overall outcome of the journey. Looking back, everything I did that was wrong was actually right in the grand scheme of things. Every mistake I made, every sin I committed, every tear I cried was perfectly done. Perfect execution. This sounds crazy, I know. But understand this. The thing about being down twenty points in a game is you can either accept the ass-whooping, or you can fight your way to a win. I was so used to losing that it became normal for me to say, "Ehh, maybe next time," to things happening in my life. I had to learn that my path to winning was going to be a little different.

I wasn't built to be the star on the team. I wasn't built to be the popular kid in school or have the freshest clothes. But with all the losses I took, I eventually realized that I was being prepared to be built differently. I was becoming something I couldn't quite understand. And if I'm being honest, I still haven't fully untapped that build, but this is what I can say. From the age of five to thirteen to twenty-five, the seed was planted: I always knew mentally I'd get somewhere far and tell the story of how I did it. I never thought I'd get the opportunity to graduate from college. Shit, with what money? I never would've even guessed I'd be a commissioned officer in the United States Navy—please, that's for middle- and upper-class folk I'd watch on TV. I never would've ever guessed that I'd start my own clothing line and trademark it. But in order for those to pop off, I had to understand my own journey from the beginning. I had to understand my purpose. I had to walk down memory lane through the ugly times and trying times to remind myself who I was, who I was built to be, and who I was built to become.

Life goes by so fast that we tend to forget the things we've been through that got us through. Oddly, I barely remember my childhood. I can recall bits and pieces, like being in Miami, Florida, playing with Power Ranger action figures in the front yard. I can't remember certain people or even being told that I was loved. But one thing I will always remember is at the age of five, my mom placed me in a car and drove almost endlessly down a long road. Turns out, we were leaving Miami and headed into a new life that I was not prepared for. But let's rewind. Let's go back five years to December 17, 1993, at 2:30 p.m.

My mom went into labor. At 4:00 p.m., I finally decided to come out and face the world after nine months of being shielded from it. I came out a beautiful, healthy baby at seven pounds eight ounces into the hands of a loving-caring parent, born into a room filled with nurses and doctors—no family or friends in sight. Among the strangers in the room, none of them looked to be my father. *That was it; you weren't there. You forgot to be there! Forget everything else. You forgot to be there. Forget the bad day you had at work that stressed you out and made you forget to be there. Forget the argument that you and Mom had a week earlier that you're still holding a grudge for, that made you forget to be there. Forget all the people who cut you off on the road that day and did you wrong that made you forget to be there. I did nothing to you! How could you not be in the hospital room to see the child you'd made come into the world?* I can imagine those being the thoughts racing through my mom's head.

Once I was pushed out, my mom grabbed me and held me close. She looked into my eyes, and I looked into hers. Right then, I knew this would be all I had to depend on. Ironically, our leaving had nothing to do with you not being there from the start or the lies and cheating because Mama still gave you a chance to be in my life. But we'll come back to that in a minute.

To make the beginning of my life even more interesting, I was born with a deformity called talipes equinovarus, commonly referred to as clubfoot. This wasn't something I was genetically passed down or anything. I just happened to be in the rare percentage of babies to be diagnosed with this deformity. Unfortunately, I was bilateral, meaning I had clubfoot in both of my feet. So both of my legs were cocked like two loaded pistols curving inward versus being naturally straight out. I guess my feet were so bad that I needed the help of surgery to assist in repairing their structure. I don't remember much from that time, but having to have surgery as a baby is pretty alarming and nerve-racking. To have to watch your young child on a surgery table have procedures performed that don't have a 100 percent success rate? I could only imagine it from that side. My mom watched my life change forever on that table.

After the surgery, for most of my toddler years, I wore orthopedic shoes to help my feet straighten out. You know, I really don't remember much of this time because I was so young. But even twenty-five years later, I still see the effects from it. I still feel the effects. It's funny how some things from the past carry on to our present. Some things you just never forget, never let go of, never move on from, never heal from, and those things stay with you every day.

There were a lot of things I thought I would never get the chance to do because of this deformity. If I hadn't healed properly or even if my mom had decided not to do anything about my clubfoot, I probably would have been permanently crippled, not able to play with other kids, run around in circles for no reason, or play basketball—or even simpler: I wouldn't be able to walk on my own will. But even this early in my life, I couldn't be stopped from what I was destined to do, who I was destined to become.

I did not realize it at the moment, but my mom would be the same lady I would one day make proud. One thing about life, the time continues to tick forward. Subconsciously, I was leaving the old me in Miami and starting a new journey that God had handcrafted for me. It wasn't always champagne and good times for this single mom and her five-year-old child. She was born and raised in Nassau, Bahamas, and left her family to try something out of the island norm, to pursue the American dream and flourish in the opportunities the United States offered people trying to better themselves. Imagine, a foreigner coming into a new country not knowing a soul, barely speaking the main language, with only a high school diploma and a child to take care of, trying to find a way.

I recall a few pieces of my childhood. While driving on that long road, I remember us pulling over into empty lots at night. I can remember my mom putting a blanket over my body so I wouldn't be cold. I thought we were making pit stops because Mommy was tired from driving until a few days passed, and we kept coming back to the same parking lot at night. Mama would say to me that everything would be all right and not to worry. I would watch her search for pennies, nickels, and dimes to feed the both of us whatever we could afford with the loose change we got. She would go without eating sometimes just to make sure I had enough. Sacrifices are what mothers make for their children no matter what. But, of course, being a child equals being selfish almost all the time and not understanding what goes into making things happen in this world. I believed my mom when she said everything would be OK. I didn't understand the predicament that we were in, sleeping in cars, barely having enough to eat at times. All I knew was that Mama and I were in this struggle together and that she loved me. Honestly, that was all I cared about. We had to endure this for my safety, for our safety.

Leaving Miami was a tough thing to do, especially with nowhere to go, but he left my mom no choice. One day, we came home after a long day to a random note left in front of the door. Believing that it was mail, she took the note inside the house and set it on the table. Now, some may call this being nosy or just plain ol' instinct, but whichever one it was that day, it probably saved our lives. She unfolded the poorly sealed note and began to read it. Turns out that this note was a threat on both our lives. An anonymous person wrote a descriptive letter about how he would kill me, my mom and grandma if he didn't pay the money he owed. I can imagine my mama being scared shitless reading that note, especially because she was completely clueless about Dad's side hustles. We wasted no time loading up the car with as much stuff as our 1993 Geo Prism could hold, and we left. We didn't look back or think twice about it. We left Miami with nowhere to go except the hell away from danger. And there we were, on the endless road with just each other in the car to keep company, to protect, to look out for, to care for, to love, and to figure out what was next.

Life deals us a deck of cards. Some people are given hands that automatically win them the game, and the other people are dealt hands that force them to work harder to try to win. Without knowing, every person on this earth is given a chance at life. Though the life we are born into isn't one we choose, we have to make the best of what we are given.

Some people are born into the families of doctors, lawyers, military officials, millionaires, and professional athletes. Other people are born into families of poverty and little to no education or into struggling and abusive homes. It's no fault of yours if you were the child born into any of those situations. But it is on you to decide which direction you will go.

The difference in being born into money and having to bust your ass for every opportunity and seat at the table is clear. People who go without most of their childhood really have the advantage in life. Sounds weird as fuck, I know, but hear me out. People born into fewer opportunities in life have no choice but to make something of ourselves, but whether you travel down the right or wrong path is what makes the difference between making it out and barely making it. Then again, the theory behind the right and wrong path is relative to what you believe to be right and wrong. For some people raised in the environment where gangbanging and selling drugs is a way of life, sometimes that is the only means to make it, to put food on the table. We watch the American dream on television—you know, graduating college; people wearing a suit to work every day; husband and wife, walking into the house saying, "Honey, I'm home!"; and having your kids rush to the door to hug you. Looks good as fuck on the TV, and I guess that's where it will stay because I have to get back to my reality. When I turn the television off, I go back to my reality, the reality of making ends meet the best way I know how.

The cycle of being disadvantaged can always be broken, but you have to want to change the way things were. The process is supposed to be ugly; it's a process. You have to want something different that will forever leave a positive imprint on this world. What's my purpose? I ask myself this question a lot, and I'm honestly still trying to figure it out. But an even better question is what's yours? Ironically, people will spend their entire lives trying to figure out the meanings and purposes of their lives.

Growing up, I was forced to understand the basis of life. Whether you were raised in a household with both parents, with one parent, or with no parents, one thing remained true, and that was you had to survive. Whether you were given the full tree or the short end of the stick, the rent was still due on the first of the month. Mama always made a way. I would never question how I got new sneakers or new clothes when I knew we did not have extra money. Honestly, I did not care. I wanted the new Jordans that came out no matter how much they cost. I wanted the new game systems. I wanted the new everything and never thought once about where the money came from to buy those things. With all the wants I had, I never thought about the fact that it takes money to make things happen. It never occurred to me that Mama working long days and nights was the way she fed us.

My mom came to the United States with a high school diploma, a heavy island accent, and no money to her name. Where are the six figures in that? She fought hard to establish herself in a new country, so one of the things she did was marry in 1991. Two years later, she gave birth to me. Now rewind to December 17, 1993, 2:35 a.m.; she held me in her arms for the first time. Her eyes roamed the delivery room to see who came in support of her second newborn child. As her eyes observed each corner of the room, there was no one in sight—no family or friends, no father. She looked back down at me in her arms and said my name. I glanced into her eyes, still screaming from the pop the doctors gave me. She looked into my eyes with tears rushing down her face. I guess from that point she knew it was only she and I on this journey together. Indeed, we were.

You read that right: I wasn't my mom's first child. She had a child by my biological father a couple of years before I came along. His name was Kevin, Kevin Butler. I never got the chance to meet him because he was called back to God within a year of being on earth. Kevin had health complications that his undeveloped body could not handle. I can't help but to feel that a part of me is missing; sometimes I feel a void. Even though I wasn't on earth yet to meet him, the hurt from losing a brother still hits me hard. Some people say, "If you never had something, you can't know how it feels to lose it." I somewhat agree, but it's funny how things you go without for long periods of time seem to remind you that you don't have them.

Every day, I look at kids who have parents, siblings, still-living grandparents, nice clothes, and what seems to be a good life. I never had those, so I can't know how it feels to lose it, right? I do, and I take that loss with me each day with the understanding that I have him as my guardian angel looking over me. Wait. It's selfish of me to only consider myself and the way I feel. What about my mom and how she felt to lose a child—her very first baby boy? I could not imagine, but she knew on December 17, 1993, that our lives would change forever, and I would come into the world for the first time. I just had to make her proud.

Picture this, when you lose something, you normally go looking for it, right? Better yet, when you finally notice that something is not with you anymore, depending on how important it is to you, you'll make a pretty big deal about not having it. I've lost something as simple as my phone before and didn't notice it was missing until I got to my car, but once I did notice it wasn't with me, I would immediately go back inside to aggressively look for my phone. It was important to me, and I couldn't go anywhere without it. Hell, just the feeling alone of not having my phone or wallet on me makes me uneasy.

Dad…you lost me, right? Did you notice I wasn't in your life anymore? Did you just get used to it? And for my grand question, did you bother to get it back? But at the same time, I don't blame you in that regard. The reason is because you don't notice that something isn't there anymore if you never realized you had it. If you love what you have lost, you do whatever you can to get it back. Right? I mean, am I trippin'? But we ain't talking about losing a phone or circling back to go home because you forgot to turn the oven off and just remembered. We ain't talking about losing a bet or remembering that the headlights are on after turning the car off. We are talking about me, a human being, your child, your son. If everything I said earlier is true, did you ever love me? You sure enough lost me but didn't do whatever you could to get me back. Sounds real as fuck when it's put like that, huh? Well, that's just a sample of how I've felt for nearly three decades and counting. But fuck all that. This isn't about you at all or how you weren't there all through the years. I just had some things to ask, some things to get off my chest. Talking about you will be the shortest chapter in this book, similar to my memories of you. Harsh, huh? Again, that's just a sample of how I've felt for nearly three decades and counting. This is about me and how I made it to become a man in this screwed-up world. And it happened without you.

There're too many good times, good memories, and good people to address to focus on the bad pieces. So in essence, I really do appreciate you because everything that has happened has shaped me to become the muthafuckin' king I am. With that, let's get to it.

CHAPTER 2

PICKING UP THE PACE

For the better part of six months, we were homeless. We slept in our car a handful of those times, in our '93 Geo Prism. But I guess even in that we were still blessed. We had a roof over our heads, the car roof. Food wasn't on the table, but we had wrappers and paper bags on the floor. Even in a shitty situation living in our car, somehow I still saw the goods. The times we didn't sleep in the car, we stayed with really nice people and their families who opened their homes to us for weeks at a time before we overstayed our welcome.

The living situation was awkward for me. I slept head to toe in other kids' beds with them. Sometimes, I just grabbed a blanket and slept on the floor. I watched the interaction between the families we would stay with and the love they had for each other. They would hug and embrace each other often. All the while, I would feel so out of place, almost as if I didn't belong there. I mean, hell, we *didn't* belong there. Whenever I felt that way, I just went and hugged my mom for comfort. That was all I had to turn to anyway.

I remember this one family we stayed with. There was this kid who wanted to show me his room all the time, as if the room changed colors every day. He wasn't showing me because he wanted me to feel welcome but as a reminder that this was his room, not mine. I grabbed my mom's keys and went to the car to sit. Well, I was in my room now, my own space. It was tough not knowing if we would have a bed to sleep in that night or if we would recline the seats back for the night. I didn't know if my next meal was going to be a hot one or if it was going to be whatever we could afford to eat with the loose pennies and nickels from the change holder.

The first time I felt pain was watching my mom go without eating for the day because of only having enough money to feed me. She would always make sure I was good before she did anything. One night, we pulled into this parking lot, and without her saying a word, I already knew we were getting ready to stay the night there. It was cold that night, like really cold that night, around forty degrees, so I went to sleep curled up, arms inside my shirt for warmth. I was content but still shivering a bit. I woke up the next morning with a blanket over me. I turned over and saw my mom sleeping with nothing giving her warmth but her breath blowing into her hands to rub her body. You talk about love and sacrifice, man. I didn't understand everything then, but now that I'm older, I get it. I understand everything to its finest detail.

Right then and there, seeing my mom like that, I understood somehow and some way, I was going to make sure she was taken care of for as long as I could breathe. But even in those weird, dreadful times, we were still blessed. Of course, things could have been better, but they could also have been a lot worse. We moved from Miami, finding ourselves in Fort Lauderdale, eventually crossing the state line into Georgia. We stayed in Coffee County for a while, which is a three-and-a-half-hour drive from the state line. Then we somehow found ourselves in Clayton County.

After about six months of my mom working part-time jobs here and there, waitress work, and saving up loose change, we got our first apartment—something finally we could call our own. It was Summerwind Drive Apartments on Tara Boulevard. I just couldn't wait to finally play at the playground with other kids.

*   *   *

I remember this time in second grade at Tara Elementary. I wasn't the most popular kid at school, but I definitely wasn't a square. I stood somewhere in the middle of the two crowds and got along with everyone for the most part. I was sitting in class, and I could not hold my bladder any longer, so I got up and went to the restroom.

As I walked into the restroom, I noticed a wet-floor sign. Whether the ground was actually wet or not, I always stepped around those signs as a just in case. Knowing my luck, it would be the one time I stepped near the wet-floor sign believing the shit was dry already, and I'd slip because it was actually wet. Nonetheless, I walked around the sign and headed straight to the stall to pee. I heard the restroom door open and close, so I assumed someone had walked in. Someone did; it was this playful-ass boy named Caleb. This kid was in my class and was known to be very annoying, but I didn't think he would try to play in the restroom where we peed.

As I was leaving the stall, he went into the stall directly next to mine. I went to the sink to wash my hands and do a quick check of my clothes, making sure I looked decent and didn't get drops of urine on me somehow, before heading back to class. Simultaneously, as I was doing this, Caleb finished doing whatever it was he went into the stall for and walked out to come by the sink. Sure enough, he began to talk shit, and he immediately became playful, shoving me and laughing. I was smiling at this point—not to entertain his playful gestures but to let him know "All right, bruh, that's enough."

After washing my hands, I didn't even bother drying them in there because I couldn't be in the restroom for another second with him playing around. I turned my back and started to damp my hands on my pants and waved them from side to side to let them air dry the rest of the way back to class. I took a couple of steps, and as I was walking out, Caleb started laughing even more, almost diabolically. I looked around and then down to see what the hell he was laughing about. Before I could plant my leg on the ground again, he pushed me from behind, and I landed face-first on the restroom floor. He pushed me right when I positioned my foot around the wet-floor sign so I had less balance to catch myself before falling.

As I was lying there, I noticed that blood was coming from my face, and I immediately started panicking, freaking out that my face was broken or some shit. I heard Caleb run out of the restroom. He left me lying there in cold blood. I finally got up from the floor, and I looked in the mirror to see the damage done. My face looked in place, but soon I noticed that the blood wasn't coming from anywhere else but my mouth. I opened it to trace where the blood was coming from. Without hesitation, I felt a chill, and my eyes zoomed in on the gap I now had in my mouth. My front right tooth was gone, only maybe one-third of the tooth was still rooted in my gums. Now, I was pissed as hell.

Even as a kid, I always analyzed situations and examined their extra components. For instance, not only was I clearly mad that this boy had pushed me by a muthafuckin' wet-floor sign, which caused me to lose my tooth, but I was equally upset at the fact that this boy ain't wash his hands before he touched me. This boy pushed me with his pissy, shitty residue-ass hands. The second thing I was in awe about was the fact that he ran out of the restroom as I was lying on the floor like a chalked crime scene outline. I felt as if this was premeditated, but I digress. As all of those thoughts raced through my head, I finally reached into the stall to get toilet paper to wipe the blood from my mouth and try to slow the active flow from my gums.

Once I got some control of the situation, I looked on the ground to find my tooth. As I was searching for it, I heard the door open, and I looked up. It was Caleb. This muthafucka came back. He came back for this ass-whooping, but with him was our second-grade teacher. I'm not sure what he told her. Maybe he told her that he walked into the restroom and noticed I was lying on the floor or some bullshit lie. But for his next move, Caleb literally got on the floor hands and knees to help me look for the tooth that he knocked out. I was looking at him as I was still on the ground, like "Dawg, what the hell is wrong with this kid?" He was literally on the floor searching. All right, whatever, he was dumb as hell for coming back to the crime scene, but he was smart as shit for bringing the teacher with him because she saved him from this ass-whooping.

After we searched for a while, the tooth came up, and of course, Caleb was the one who found it. The murderer. I snatched it from him and confused as to what I was supposed to do with it now, so I put it in my pocket. Now that my tooth was missing from my mouth, all I wanted to do was get it fixed somehow. My mom couldn't get me from school because of work, so I went the entire day in class, lunch, walking to the bus stop with no teeth. Yeah, I am being very dramatic. I had teeth, but with my front one pretty much missing, I might as well have been missing all of them.

Later that afternoon, I got on the bus, and my mom saw that my tooth was gone from my mouth and lost her mind. This is something I still have to live with to this day. My front right tooth is not my natural tooth because it was knocked out in second grade. I went to the dentist, and they put a cap over the remaining tooth to fill in the void. Moral of the story, there are some things that happened to you or affected you years ago, but somehow you are reminded of them every day of your life. Question is though, will you let those events take over your life, or will you embrace them and continue to move forward?

*   *   *

Early one Saturday morning, my mom came into my room to wake me up by saying, "Let's go! Get up! We have errands to run."

Being the obedient ten-year-old boy I was, I got up, brushed my teeth, got dressed, and walked out the door to meet my mom outside. We got into our car and drove away to handle business for the day. I always went with her on errands and tasking runs she had to do. I thought that I always had to go with her everywhere because I wasn't old enough to be in the house by myself. Better yet, I thought it was probably because she did not want me burning the house down trying to cook noodles while she was gone. But this particular day, I realized the bigger purpose.

We finally reached the first stop of our adventurous day of errands. As we came around to the parking spot, my mom put the car in park. I looked up, and we were in front of this white building. I couldn't make out the name of the place, but I noticed a long line that wrapped outside the building. In my mind, I said, *Man, Mama could have left me home for this.* We got out of the car to join this never-ending line. I was still confused on where we were and what we were doing there. An hour and a half went by, and we eventually reached the front of the line.

Finally! Now we're just waiting for the next available clerk to call us up. Eventually, we were up next, and the clerk signaled us to the front.

As we walked quickly to the counter, I noticed my mom pull out folders with paperwork inside of them, nearly the size of a medium-length history textbook. I wasn't sure, but it looked important. I began to listen to the dialogue between them. They started to talk about food. What this sounded like to a ten-year-old kid listening in was a food conversation that I could've stayed in the car for. At this point I was saying to myself, *I know this lady did not bring me out this early in the morning to talk to a stranger about food.*

So now I was upset, standing to the side of my mom with a slight attitude. None of this made any sense in my mind. Ten minutes went by, and they were still talking about food, except this time I noticed a change in tone in my mom's voice. She must have really felt strongly about this nutrition debate. Thirty seconds passed, and as I stood there, I could see and hear the trembling in her voice. I looked around to quickly observe my surroundings. I saw other people in the building and other kids with their parents. I finally looked up at a sign label by the door that read "Division of Family and Children Services," also known as the Welfare Office. I didn't know a lot about Welfare at all except that it was for poor people who needed financial help.

When I realized where I was, I hung my head down, feeling ashamed. During this time period, to be a recipient of food stamps wasn't necessarily a cool thing, nor were they as easily accessible to people. For me, that meant that we needed assistance from the government to eat, to survive. I processed this in a matter of seconds, and I wasn't sure how to feel. What would the kids at school say about me if they found out I lived off food stamps? I looked up, and my mom turned away from the counter as they ended the conversation. She grabbed my hand, and we walked out of the building.

I didn't know what to say, whether to comfort her in the situation with "I love you" or shut up because I could make the situation worse. But we drove back home, and my mom began to talk to me about life. We always had talks like this, even when I was too young to really comprehend things. She always told me that things would eventually click once I got older and had more experiences. In this particular life talk, she told me that everything was going to be all right and that we were going to make it. I was still puzzled by what had happened at the Welfare Office but too uneasy to ask what had gone down.

She finally told me. She said that we had applied for food stamps because the cost of living was becoming very pricey for our income. Simply put, my mom was doing the best she could. As I continued to listen, not really understanding everything she was saying, she said that we did not qualify for food assistance.

I said, "Wait, ma. What?"

Now I was really confused. Being new on the job driving the school buses, she only brought home about $24,000 a year, a little less than that after taxes, which I thought was a lot of money still. I was sadly mistaken, especially when you have bills and a roof and food to provide for not only yourself but a child. I looked to the left and to the right, and I saw no one to help us, so we had to do for ourselves. With an unsteady voice, she uttered, "We were five dollars over the required salary to receive food stamps."

Tears streamed from her face—and mine too. Everything just seemed to be going against us. I asked my mom, "Why me? Why us? Why can't we be rich?" and all the questions anyone would ask randomly when things are going wrong.

She grabbed me, brought me in close, and responded by saying, "Son, I can't answer that. But what I can tell you is that you don't need to worry because I am following someone much bigger and better than all of our problems. Just know you are going to make something great of yourself. We will be all right."

All I could say was "OK," and we continued to hug and embrace each other. And of course, life goes on.

* * *

Random injection—buying batteries was always a tedious and irrelevant part of our expenses. If batteries stopped working in my house, either we tried to get more use out of them, or I wasn't using whatever I needed batteries for. Anytime the remote controller—or as some urban folks would pronounce it, the "mote"—or my video game would stop working because of the batteries, we had a couple of home remedies to get some more juice out of them. One thing I would do was grab the mote from the top and slap the ass end on my hand repeatedly. I hoped by doing so that I would knock some reserved juice into the batteries so they could work. Usually after slapping the batteries a couple of times, I would get two or three clicks to work before they died again.

The next step was to take the batteries and put them in the freezer. I'm not sure if this was just tribal knowledge, but I thought putting batteries in the freezer for a couple of hours would add more life to them. I figured the longer the batteries were in the freezer, the longer they could recharge and be used.

Whether any of these really worked is still a mystery, but we did what we did to make things work somehow. What can I say? We did what we did to save money.

*   *   *

Before cell phones and electronics occupied kids' time, going outside to play was our fun. Meeting up with friends down the street to walk the block and roast each other was our social club. We even had our own backyard sports arena. We played football, basketball, ghetto soccer (I'll explain what that is in a minute), backyard track and field, you name it. Finding a source of entertainment every day after school and on the weekends was a great time, and I always had fun. We played this one game with a football we called "throw 'em up, buss 'em up." Essentially, this was a full-contact game with no pads or bodily protection. When playing this game, you had two options: either you ran as fast as you could with the football with everyone chasing you down to kill you, or to avoid contact completely, you'd throw the ball in the air and allow someone else the chance to put his life on the line.

That was just one of many games we played down South, but one particular Saturday, my friends and I decided to play baseball. We made up where first, second, and third bases and home plate would be and how far out, using sticks or whatever we could find. Now that I think about it, we didn't use baseball mitts, because we didn't own any. We used rusted old bats we would find and a dirty baseball one of the kids randomly had. Now I know what you are probably thinking, that this is extremely dangerous and, more obvious, extremely dumb. No gloves, no helmets, no face shields, just a rusted bat and our bare hands to catch the ball. Funny enough, this was normal for us back then. This was what we did because unlike today, when kids can't wait to go inside and play video games or hop on social media, we couldn't wait to get home and go outside to play, and we played hard until the apartment lights came on.

The time we played baseball was so much fun, and I'll never forget it. There were roughly ten of us playing, so we spilt the teams up to have five versus five. My team was the first up to bat. Three of my friends went before me and hit the ball so hard it damn near smacked the kid who was pitching. I was up fourth to bat, with the bases fully loaded. They were all counting on me to bring them on home—no pressure. I grabbed the bat, and up until this point, I had never gripped a baseball bat ever. I wasn't sure how I was supposed to stand. I wasn't sure where my hands were supposed to be on the bat or where I should hit the ball. My brain was so disorganized, but my face didn't show the confusion.

I got up to the home plate ready to hit this muthafuckin' home run. Dieon, who was the pitcher, threw the ball. It was clearly overthrown at least two feet to my right side, but I still moved my arms forward to swing and to try knocking the ball out of the yard. Strike one. The ball rolled into the street. We got it back and reset. He threw the ball again. This time, it was a pretty good throw down the middle. I swung wildly and missed the ball terribly. Strike two. As I mention the first and second strike, I am not referring to what a strike means in the baseball world. I'm talking about me. I had two attempts to realize I didn't know what I was doing and to put that damn bat down. I knew I didn't know how to handle the baseball bat, swinging wild and awkwardly the first two times. I didn't put it down. I kept going because I was no punk bitch.

Dieon set up again to the throw the baseball, and all that was running through my head was that I was about to hit this home run. He threw the ball, another one like the first pitch, and it was way off. I said, "Fuck that!" and went to hit the ball. I swung the bat with all of the strength inside me, and as I let the forward motion of the bat carry my arms. I lost control of the bat, but instead of letting it go, I held on. The bat came around toward my face, hit my forehead, and knocked me out cold. There I was, lying down on the grass, looking around with a massive headache. My friends helped me up and, surprisingly, walked with me back to my house. Usually, when anything bad happened to one of us as kids, the first instinct was to laugh at that person. So for them to help me instead of laughing like hyenas was unexpected.

I finally got home, and as I walked through the door, my mom almost instantly noticed something was wrong with me—she probably saw the tears streaming down my face at this point. She started yelling at me aggressively, "What happened, boy?" multiple times.

I was embarrassed to tell her what had actually happened, so my first instinct was to lie—not lie *completely* though. I planned to still incorporate the baseball bat into my story but instead say that I was in the midst of being a hero, trying to stop an all-out brawl between some strangers on the way home, and got hit with a baseball bat as collateral.

After her asking what had happened for the tenth time, I finally responded by saying, "I hit myself with a baseball bat, Ma," while wiping away the last tear that fell from my eye. How embarrassing is that? I knew that my made-up story wasn't going to work, so I just told the truth. I was also urging her to stop yelling because my head was killing me. When I told her what really happened, her concerned "What happened to my sweet baby boy?" demeanor changed to a facial expression of "This stupid-ass boy." She told me to go into the bathroom and wait for her.

She went into the kitchen. When she came into the bathroom, she had a bag of frozen green beans to put on my forehead, to help calm the headache, I thought. We didn't always have an icemaker or ice tray, so we treated swelling, wounds, and scars with whatever we had. And of course, we ate those green beans later that night. The entire time I was in the bathroom, I had yet to look at myself in the mirror. This entire time, I thought the frozen bag was because I had complained about the headache. I look up at myself in the mirror, and my eyes opened wide. After taking a deep breath, I whispered, "Fuck, fuck, fuck, fuck, fuck!" in panic to myself. My mom was in the next room when I whispered those irreligious words to myself. I had a giant-ass knot the size of a plump tomato on my forehead. I didn't feel it initially on my forehead when I was outside, and none of my friends said anything while walking me home. I was even more surprised because they didn't laugh at me, at this fat-ass knot. Thanks, old friends, for not laughing at me.

One of my biggest realizations was baseball would not be the sport for me. The swelling went down after a week or so, and I was back outside on the prison fields playing "throw 'em up, buss 'em up."

Oh yeah, ghetto soccer—I didn't forget to explain what it is. Ghetto soccer was a game of soccer mixed with rugby, football, and I believe medieval horse racing. Just know that when we played that, we would have to stop the game because someone got hit too hard. I am thankful none of the times we played and stopped was because of me—well, except for baseball.

* * *

What may seem out of the ordinary to some people is ordinary for others. What some could see as struggling could be the way of life for another. Having an important person missing from your growing process to some may be detrimental and a progress stopper. Others don't really notice; they adapt. I always found the simple things in life to be sufficient, and that was because of the tremendously simple life I lived. And you know what? It didn't bother me at all. It was what I knew.

One day, my mom and I were out running errands. I pretty much followed her everywhere she went when I was young. I can remember this great day in Georgia because it was hot as hell. Georgia heat is like no other—the dry, humid hot that gives you swamp ass thirty minutes into the day after leaving your house. Well, this day was no different, but the heat has nothing to do with this story I'm getting ready to tell you. This is just a quick rant about how hot it was that day.

The air conditioner had stopped working in our car, so as we drove around the city, we had to roll the windows down to try to cool off. We had one of the cars where the air conditioner didn't work, but the heater worked just fine. The heater could melt metal, but that helped us none living in a state where it's hot the majority of the year. Even though we had the windows down, the hot air from outside mixed with the heat from the engine just made it hell.

We rode in silence most times. It was just too damn hot to even speak to each other on scorching days like those.

Quick sidetrack—my mom was great. Well, I guess this is the second sidetrack because I started talking about how hot Georgia was. Just bear with me. I would watch TV and see how families would have college and tuition bank accounts set up for their kids. It made sense. As a parent, you want to give them the best opportunity at accelerating their education at a higher-learning institution. Honestly, that is how any parent should want to set their kids up to excel and give them options. However, again, what may seem out of the ordinary to some people is ordinary for others. For some parents, it is completely normal to fulfill those promises for their kids. For others, you simply do what you can. My college fund was placed in a closet, buried under some unworn clothes. That was for security reasons. If someone broke into our apartment, it wouldn't be completely obvious to see. My college fund wasn't a briefcase filled with thousands of dollars. This was a milk carton, which once had milk inside of it, now bleached and cleaned out to remove the odor. My college fund was filled with pennies, nickels, dimes, and quarters. You could still clearly see the residue paper leftover from the "Reduced Milk" label being ripped off the front. My mom renamed it with black permanent marker, "Don't Touch." Yep, don't freakin' touch. Where did she get money to put inside my milk carton account? Easy, if we got fast food and paid with cash, the spare change was headed to my fund. If we were walking on the sidewalk, and I just happened to glance down and see change lying on the concrete, it was going to my milk carton account. That was how we supported my college fund, though it seemed so far away I never really took the college route seriously anyway. I wholeheartedly believed college was something every kid was supposed to consider because you were supposed to. But ultimately, it seemed like a fantasy. We did what we could. She did what she had to with what she had, and I love her to the moon and back for it.

OK, I'm done with my two quick sidetracks. Now back to the original story I wanted to share. We got to the gas station on this hot Georgia day. I always pumped the gas when I rode with my mom, and nothing was different about this time. As I got out of the car, I forgot to grab the money from her to pay for the gas. I said to my mom from the window, "Ma, how much you want me to put on pump three?"

She reached her arm toward the backseat and went under her chair to grab something. I assumed it was for her purse to get money out. She pulled her arm up, and in her hand was the milk carton account, which was once nearly filled to the top at one point. Watching her raise the cartoon up, it was now almost half empty. I couldn't believe what I was seeing, mainly because the damn cart said, "Don't Touch." Then I noticed the "Don't Touch" once written on the front had been crossed out. She looked at me, and I looked at her with uninterrupted eye contact for a couple of seconds. She could see the way I felt on my face.

After taking a deep breath, she said, "Baby, we gotta do what we gotta do. I'll make it up to you."

Was I upset? Hell, yeah. I thought I was going to use that money for college. I definitely didn't want to add extra stress and pressure on my mom. But I was forced to mature fast and early, so I understood why. I understood that we needed to do what we had to. I understood that I couldn't plan for the future if I didn't survive now. The milk carton was half empty, so I realized that this wasn't the first time the money had been used. She put the carton in her lap and then reached into the arm-rest and pulled out paper coin rollers. She proceeded to tilt the carton on its side so that the change could come out.

After a solid two minutes, she had enough change from it to make fifteen dollars out of pennies and dimes. Gas was about a dollar and twenty cents per gallon for unleaded regular, so the fifteen dollars would last us a week or two. Stunned by the process, I took the coined-rolled money from her and walked inside the gas station to pay for the gas. While I stood in line, I was so embarrassed. I watched the three people in front of me pay with debit cards and cash. I finally got to the cashier and asked for fifteen on pump three. I can remember this so vividly.

He asked, "OK, little man, is this gonna be cash or card?"

I responded by saying absolutely nothing. I reached into my pocket and grabbed at least eight rolled coins in the amount of fifteen dollars and put them on the counter. He looked down at the payment and then at me and said, "I understand kid."

No, he didn't. I felt somewhat ashamed and left without a receipt. I walked back to the car and pumped fifteen dollars' worth of gas into the car, and we drove off.

A lot of things like that happened in my life. I had to draw my own conclusions as to why they were happening the way they were to me. I am thankful for that experience. I learned something that day. Apparently, there is beauty in the struggle. The rain makes you appreciate the sunshine. Good times don't come without understanding what the bad times feel like. You'll appreciate those much more.

One thing I can't help but note is how fearless my mom was. Essentially down and relying on loose change to help us stay alive, she never once blamed me. When things get rough, blaming others for low points and misfortunes in your life is usually the immediate reaction. People would rather guilt-trip others, cuss folks out, and look down on people's blessings instead of taking responsibility for their own life and why it's not where they want it. I came up with this saying in early 2020, once I understood that my destiny and my blessings were all up to me. I could no longer accuse others or my situation for me not being able to make progress. The quote goes like this: "If you blame someone else for not being successful, you weren't ready to make it." Now reread it, think about it, and process it, because it's right as fuck. The sooner you take ownership of your life, understanding that each trial and lesson presented to *you* is for *you* and your growth, the better off you will be.

I never once blamed you, Ma. Give me a quick second. Let me address my mom personally. I never despised or hated you for how I grew up. You raised me the best you could, the best way you knew how with the knowledge you had, with the education you had—and, more important, with the heart you had. The reason I think I am in a good position in life today is because of one particular lesson I took from you. That was to never give up. The phrase "never give up" is used often, and you probably hear it even more. But if you truly commit those words to your journey, to *never give up*, *never*, then you will actually surpass the goals you set for yourself and you'll see how well you can perform. Just be ready.

Letter to My Mom
Dear Dianne Butler,

> Against all odds, I stand here today able to
> Live the life you always imagined for me. You
> Are the reason I stand tall and fear nothing but
> God. You have kept me guided in the right direction
> And I thank you. I can never forget you.

> Love Always,
> Your Son

It's interesting when you think about how life is seemingly better for other people, while you have to sit back and get it the hard way. I can remember being in middle school—one of the most trying times in a kid's life. It's trying because kids are mean as hell. I would get talked about and made fun of because of the nice clothes and brand-name stuff I didn't have. It's funny, I would wear Bugle Boy shirts with a pair of baggy jeans, like really baggy, loose-ass jeans, and a pair of all-purpose shoes from Payless, pretty much on a regular basis. I called them all-purpose because I wore one pair of shoes pretty much every day for everything, even my goto's on the weekends.

I remember ending the fall semester of my sixth-grade year; as a kid, all I looked forward to was Christmas and getting new clothes and shoes so I could stunt on all the kids at school. Mom did her best, but money was tight, especially around the holidays, and bills still had to be paid. The Christmas break flew by, and I was in the new semester—a New Year with last year's clothes. I remember getting off the bus and walking to homeroom, seeing everyone flaunting their new outfits as if they were auditioning for *America's Next Top Model*.

I finally got to homeroom, and I watched my entire class walk in with the newest Jordans that normally would come out around Christmastime, new Girbaud Jeans, and clean white tees. One of the worst feelings in my life was being looked at as disgusting or not cool enough because of material things I didn't have. At the same time, I never showed my emotions in public. One of my classmates asked me why I wasn't wearing any of my new clothes. He asked it assuming that I had new things to wear, like everyone's situation was the same. In my mind, I was saying to myself, "Man, I ain't got shit new," but I usually played stuff off well.

I replied by saying, "Man, I'm just lettin' y'all wear all y'all's new clothes first. I'ma wear mines later, so I'm the freshest man in the school."

Everyone appeared to be doing better than I was. When I finally got some time to myself in the restroom later, I cried in the stall—not for being teased or talked about but because I was mad at myself. I was mad at my mom. I was mad and tired of being broke. I was mad at God! I just could not comprehend why I had to be the one not able to afford nice things or to have to use layaway all the time. It was very disheartening for me because I just wanted to be accepted socially. I never personally asked my mom "Why us?" or "Why are we less fortunate?" because I knew she would slap the black off me. I sucked it up because I knew she was doing the best she could with one income. For that reason, I never complained publicly.

* * *

I went to school in Clayton County when I moved to Georgia, but after a couple of years of living in the ClayCo, we moved a county over. Mom worked as a public-school bus driver in that area, and she drove through some tough neighborhoods, picking up and dropping off kids who gang-banged and made plays throughout Atlanta. She saw that and wanted to do her best to keep me shielded from a negative lifestyle as much as possible. For that reason, we moved to Henry County, and as a result, we normally had to wake up a little earlier in order to be on time to work and school.

My mornings normally started with waking up around 3:30 a.m. I went from brushing my teeth, getting dressed, and grabbing something to eat to hopping on the 285 to commute thirty minutes. Sometimes those thirty minutes turned into an hour, depending on how bad traffic was early that morning. Georgia folk cannot drive. Nevertheless, each morning was a task in itself before the day even started. We could not afford to lose this job. This income was all that we had to keep a roof over our heads, so me understanding that, even at my young age, was imperative. There was no such thing as oversleeping or getting dressed late. Time was literally money. I made sure I was dressed and at the door on time because of all the things we had to deal with. Being late just wasn't an option. We would both be ass out, then what? No family here, all of that was in Nassau, so we had to execute perfectly.

We drove that raggedy 1993 Geo Prism for the longest time but eventually got a somewhat reliable car during my middle school years when we got the 2003 Alero. A lot of mornings, we could depend on the car not starting. Just our luck, which actually caused us to be late a number of times.

* * *

I was a good kid for the most part. I never really got into trouble at school besides being told to be quiet in class while the teacher was talking or even at times trips to the silent lunch table. I never saw getting in trouble as being cool, nor did I care to be accepted by kids who did. Being involved in various clubs and organizations kept me out of a lot what I called "experimental trouble."

At that young age, you begin to experiment and try different things. A lot of kids started drinking, having sex, smoking cigarettes—hell, smoking weed—and acting rebellious. Being a rebel and disrespectful was not my thing for some reason. In middle school, I had been pressured to try weed, sell it, drink alcohol, skip class, and do all of the things cool kids were doing.

But I chose not to. There was no real satisfaction from doing any of those besides being accepted in the eyes of others and not being called lame. Some would argue and say that I haven't lived because I haven't fallen into pressure to do things. I'd argue that you haven't lived until you've had complete control of your life and the decisions you make. Doing what you want to do and not doing what other people pressure you to do is another level of satisfaction, and I call it owning your life. I developed a motivation when I was about eleven or twelve. I vowed that I would do whatever I had to do to make a better life for myself and my family, to do that with swagger and ultimately be true to myself. I held true to that before I really understood the way I moved. I felt I had a bigger purpose when it was all said and done. I understood this at an early age. Why force trouble on myself at school when I got troubles at home? I got real-life shit to deal with at the crib.

I had already seen what struggling was. I'd lived struggling and pain. I'd lived being without a father in my life. That was enough pressure to mature a kid quick. Although I was without a father physically, I was never without a father. I wasn't the most religious person but I learned that when my father left my life, that exact moment was when God took me up under his wings personally. It was more than just going to school, being in different clubs and organizations—I felt my purpose in life was being spoken over me.

At the time, I didn't know what it was, but I could distinguish a change in my maturity level. It was time to go to work and make plans to ensure I would be successful.

CHAPTER 3

WHAT'S NEXT?

Having success is a blend between working your ass off to be where you want to be, being at the right place at the right time, and building that network of individuals who know what you bring to the table. Through the entirety of this writing, there were a lot of trials, some of which I have talked about and others I haven't mentioned yet. All happened in my life that I could have used as an excuse to stay still. I could've easily said to myself, "You know what bruh, I ain't have no daddy growing up," and turned to the streets to fill that gap missing out of my life. But I didn't; I turned my head up to the heavens and asked God to walk with me every day. I could've used my mom not graduating college and turned to the Streets University for an education. But I didn't. She sacrificed her life, dreams, and aspirations to take a chance on my future to make sure I had enough to make something of myself.

Coming up, college was never really realistic to me. I mean, don't get me wrong; I was a smart kid growing up. In elementary and middle school, I tried to make A's and B's because that was the kind of thing I was supposed to do. You are supposed to do that as a kid. I wasn't doing shit else. I was supposed to get the citizenship awards, A/B honor roll awards, perfect attendance awards, and all. Plus, I wanted my mom to come to the awards ceremonies and have something to clap for. It put a smile on my face to hear my mom say, "Great job, baby." This was when it was cool to make good grades, sit in front of the class, and get upset when you weren't called on to answer a question. Then as time went on, the standards changed, but my mind-set remained the same. Just Follow me, it'll all make sense.

For the most part, I was usually well groomed. I never really could grow facial hair because it wasn't in my genetics to have a beard or chin strap, so I always had a hairless face. I usually kept a low haircut and got it cut roughly every two weeks. This wasn't because I stayed with the fresh fades and shit from the barbershop. My mom was my barber; she cut my hair—for a while, at least six years.

Over the years, my head had been used, abused, cut, and sliced as I let her trim my head. We just didn't have the money to support fifteen-, twenty-dollar haircuts from a barber, so we made an investment in buying thirty-dollar clippers to keep me groomed. When it was time for me to get a haircut, we would set up shop either outside by the front door or inside the bathroom. I remember my mom cutting my hair for the very first time with those clippers and not using a guard. With no past barbering experience or technique at all, this lady cut my hair on prayers that she didn't mess me up too much.

Besides the wounds on and around my ears and forehead here and there, mom's haircuts got me through. I did not know anything about barbershop etiquette, but now looking back, I realize the clippers she would use to cut my hair were the same clippers she used to line me up. Hmmmmmm, I knew something wasn't right then, but I digress now. That really would explain the multiple cuts and bloodshed I endured during my home-made haircuts. I just knew haircuts weren't supposed to be painful, but in the end, we did what we had to do.

Almost all of my younger years, I had my hair cut at home, but at some point, enough was enough. I was tired of getting crooked and subpar line-ups, so I decided to act. Now check out this story: this was 2009. I was in ninth grade, and I found myself in dire need of a haircut. Mom was working a late field trip, and by the time we got home, it was too late to bother her about cutting my hair anyway. So I decided to take matters into my own hands by taking the clippers into my own hands. Yes, with no YouTube tutorial because that was still a new thing or experience cause I had never done this before, I was getting ready to perform a self-made haircut. My head was that bad, to the point I resorted to this. I had an afro that literally looked like I was straight out of a '70s R&B group, so this had to go.

I went and found the one set of clippers we owned, and at this point, I didn't understand the purpose of using a guard or the difference in haircut clippers and lineup clippers. And the simply fact that you don't use one for both purposes. The set we owned was all-in-one inclusive—it wasn't really all-in-one, but we used it like that. I plugged in the clippers, and the initial vibration coming from it made me nervous as hell. But I needed to do something about my head right then. I picked the clippers up and put them near the middle of my head to start the top-down motion. Without a guard, I put the clippers to my hair and began cutting. I put my head down, closed my eyes, and took the clippers down the right side of my head. If I could spell the sound the clippers made initially, I would probably spell it out like this: *schroooom*. I have no idea why the hell I closed my eyes, especially having live, active clippers on my head, but it was a natural reaction. I opened my eyes and saw the first clump of hair rolled up, sitting on the counter.

Nervous as hell still, I look up at the mirror in front of me and noticed a couple of things. For one, the anxiety and shaking of my hand added extra wrist weight while cutting the first row of my head. So essentially, I cut too deep. I cut my hair lower than I intended. At this point, I realized that I would have to cut the rest of my hair this exact same length all around, with no guard. Attempting to maintain the same wrist strength and concentration it took to cut the first row, I placed the clippers toward the middle of my head again and worked my way down. *Schroooom.* With my eyes closed and head down again, once I realized I had cut the second row, I opened my eyes and quickly noticed I fucked something up. The ball of hair that fell off was significantly larger than the first clump of hair resting on the counter. In a panic, I immediately looked up at the mirror and began whispering, "Fuck, fuck, fuck, fuck, fuck." I looked stupid as hell. One side of my head was medium trim, the middle of my head was damn near skinned, and the other side was still untouched.

At this stage, I had no idea what I should do. The obvious answer was to just cut all of my hair off and rock the bald look for a few weeks until my hair grew back. Yeah, no. This was 2009, and I went to school in ClayCo. In short, kids were ruthless and showed no mercy when it came to roasting, and I knew I would be slaughtered if I showed up to school with my head looking the way it did. I was already tall, dark-skinned, and 130 pounds dripping wet. So I knew if I added a bald head to that combination and had the nerve to show up to school with that appearance, I would have gotten my ass lit up. Fuck the jokes, the other kids probably would've thought I was dying and still roasted me. Kids are mean as hell.

So with that, the choice was easy for me. I stopped. My head was not finished, but I didn't want to continue screwing it up more than it already was trying to fix it somehow. I looked at myself in the mirror. I had a bootleg George Jefferson front fade. I knew this was terrible and was an awful idea from start, but now I was thinking of ways to minimize the jokes I knew were coming.

"The only part that is really messed up is the front, so if I show people the back of my head all day for a couple weeks or until the front is back proportional, I should be good." This was the pep talk I gave myself. That was my plan, to show the other kids the back and sides of my head all day. If I was holding conversation, it wouldn't be for long, and I would only turn to show the back aspect of my head. Oh, and I planned to wear a hat too. *This could work*, I thought. Time to execute the plan.

I woke up the next morning really early, like 3:00 a.m., because I wanted to see how bad my head actually was after a night's sleep. Looking in the mirror, I realized it was just as bad as the first time I saw it and for sure didn't get any better through the night. I was so embarrassed, and I could not go to school that day because I knew I would not make it through the day. So, before my mom could realize I was up, I quietly ran back to my bed, threw the covers over my entire body, and pretended to be sick. About twenty minutes later, my mom came into the room, and I acted so well I impressed myself. She bought off on the idea I was sick and allowed me to stay home.

Once she had left the house to go to work, I scrambled to search for anything my mom had in her hair-care products basket that would help me grow hair overnight. I stumbled on pink lotion, different kinds of shampoo and conditioners, and grease but nothing that could aid my hair-loss situation. I looked in the cabinet and finally came across a product that advertised essentially the quick growth of hair, very similar to Rogaine.

For twelve straight hours, only breaking for food and naps, I applied the hair-growth serum aggressively over the thinner parts of my hair while my mom was at work. I figured if I could grow four inches of hair by sunset, I could start over and have better luck just evening out my head that way. I applied it immediately over the top of my head and I used a lot, probably too damn much but it didn't matter, this was an emergency. I put a stocking cap over my head to allow the product to simmer in and formulate—not because that was what the directions told me to do but because I thought it made sense. The directions actually advised against how much I was applying to my head, but this was an extreme situation so I ignored it. Ironically, throughout the first and last time I applied it, I never once looked at my head when I took the stocking cap off to reapply more.

At this point, I was trusting the process. My tenth and final time putting the hair-growth serum on my head was thirty minutes before my mom came home. What I didn't mention though was this. When my mom came into the room that morning, it was dark so she had yet to see this fucked-up haircut I gave myself. By the time she got home from work and opened the front door, I was back in bed playing sick, with round ten of the hair-growth product applied to my head and my stocking cap on. She came straight into my room to check on me, and there I was lying down, lying. I pretended to be feeling much better after an entire day of taking medicine and resting. All was well, except my hair, but I was praying after an entire day of self-medicating my head, I would wake up with a full head of hair. I woke up the next morning to get ready for school.

Even if my head didn't fully do what I needed it to, I knew I couldn't play sick back to back, so everything I did the previous day had to work. I went into the bathroom and looked at the stocking cap. You could obviously see my head was still disproportionate in the cap. I still had faith. I slowly took the stocking cap off my head. There was no progress made. It looked the exact same as when I first screwed it up. I was mad as hell, and my first thought was to blame that hair-growth product.

"This hair-growth product is a liar, false advertisement."

That thing read "hair growth in a matter of moments." Moments must have meant in a "few weeks" because my head showed no momentary results. Well, fuck me. I got dressed, threw my skullcap on, and walked out the door to go to school.

As I was walking into school, since it was unusual for me to wear hats or anything really on my head, my friends asked me why I had one on. Plus, no "head wear" was allowed indoors. I responded to people who asked me, "I'm trying out a new look," or some smooth response along those lines.

I made it through lunch with no problem. After lunch was my fourth-period class, where I normally sat in the middle row. Class started, and thirty minutes went by without the teacher noticing me or the hat on my head. I realized I was bringing too much attention to myself by laughing at the common class distractions and back-of-the-class jokes. I must've laughed out loud hard as fuck because the teacher immediately locked eyes with me and eventually spotted the hat on my head.

Without hesitating or even asking why I had a hat on my head, she told me to remove my cap. The attention of the entire classroom was now focused on me, revealing my damn head. I knew it was over for me, but I also knew it was only a matter of time before I would have to face my fate. I sat in the middle row of class so the back of the classroom could see the uncut part of my head, but the front of the classroom would see the obvious fuck-up I did to myself. There is no easy way to remove a Band-Aid, so I took my cap off with no strategy or dramatic pause.

I just took it off my head. Immediately, I heard ten voices yell, "Dammnnnnnnnnnn!" Those voices came from the kids up front who saw it first. At this point, I was embracing the embarrassment I knew would eventually come. I could hear chairs rumble behind me, from the kids in the back of the classroom scrambling to see what was so funny.

The twelve kids sitting behind me flew to the front of the class and began laughing dramatically, literally rolling on the fuckin' floor and crying from laughing so hard. I'm not sure why some part of me expected the teacher to intervene and help me—you know, tell the students to "sit down now" or threaten them with detention or some shit. None of that happened, and now that I think about it, she really stared at my haircut in disbelief while the class was crying their eyes out. She either couldn't believe how quickly the other kids rearranged the classroom to laugh at me, or she couldn't believe that I had the nerve to come to school with this fucked-up haircut thinking I wasn't going to be exposed. Whatever the case, I knew this was only the beginning of the worst day of my life—first, because I still had a solid three hours of school left, and second, because I was now going to walk the halls with the upperclassmen witnessing my George Jefferson haircut. After this day, I vowed never to cut my own hair again. I guess you can say I learned my lesson.

*   *   *

My mom and I made a trip just about every year for several years back to Nassau, Bahamas, to spend time with family. I remember I used to always go to the airport dressed up. Never once did I ever travel in sweats, shorts, or relaxing clothes like the other kids at the airport were traveling. I usually wore slacks, a buttoned-collar shirt, and dress shoes. Ready to go. Now, I wasn't dressed this way to impress people at the terminals, nor was it to create an image that we had it like that. When we flew, we were always on buddy passes. From what I understood about them, the seniority of the person who worked for the airline you received buddy passes through determined your priority to get on the flight. Oh, and they were cheap cheap. But, of course, cheap tickets came at a cost in themselves, and we were on standby with other people traveling with the same passes. I guess they had better luck than we did. We usually had low priority. So while we were at the airport, we had to pay close attention to the screen and to our names potentially being called at the terminal.

One time, there was one seat left on the plane back to Atlanta from the Bahamas and it was my mom and I left. I thought she was going to leave my ass there at the airport to catch the flight. She stayed though and let this guy traveling by himself go.

Back to the part of me always being dressed up in slacks and a button-up. Because we always flew on buddy passes, open seats on flights could be anywhere, and sometimes they were in first class. From what I remember, first class sometimes had a dress code—or at least that's what my mom taught me. So we couldn't risk not making a flight, especially coming back home, because we weren't dressed appropriately if seats opened up. So we were casket sharp at the airport. There were a few times we had been back and forth at the airport at least five times because each of the other times we went, the flight was full. Gotta love those buddy passes.

*   *   *

As the times changed and I grew older, I grew. I learned that my mom could only push me so far in life until I had to find strength to push myself.

In high school, I can remember it well. I was in ninth grade, and the school bell rang to let us go home for the day. You know that feeling you get before a fight starts? How it suddenly gets quiet and then random noises begin to break out? Almost as if I sensed it coming, I walked outside to catch the bus home, and it went dead silent for three seconds. It's like time slowed down for those few seconds. The next thing I heard was yelling from the crowd that quickly formed and punches being thrown.

Now, it wasn't unusual at all for a fight to happen and be accompanied by local gangs at the schools in ClayCo. At least two happened every week. I turned and looked back at the fight as I continued to walk to my bus to not get caught up in the crowd. And just like that, it hit me. Not a fist, not a gang member. Reality. Reality hit me so hard, and I began to analyze what was really going on around me. I noticed that the local gang members who were inciting the fight had graduated from the school years ago. They would come back for football and basketball games, hang out on the school yard, talk to the younger girls, and smoke weed, and it seemed like they would recruit the young high school boys to fuck with them, especially once school dismissed us.

That's what this is, I said in my mind. Those young kids were fighting their way into gang life. I sat on the bus as police began to respond and scatter the crowd. I had witnessed these kinds of fights happen often, but for some reason, this hit me a little different. After seeing that go down, I knew I didn't want to end up like that. Not even focusing on the gang-initiation part, I didn't want to be the guy who graduated and did nothing with his life. That was my eye-opener that I needed to witness—not the fight itself but the negative influences that others provide when they haven't been shown a better way out, a better way to win. That cycle was going to break with me. Instead of being mad and spiteful when negative things happened in my life, I decided that I was gonna stay true, smile, and show love regardless of the situation.

I went harder after that day, game planning on the future and understanding that I was going somewhere in life with purpose. I just had to trust the process. I had to trust God that every obstacle he put in the way was for my personal growth. I had to trust God that when my mom said I couldn't hang out with a certain group of friends or go to house parties that it was to protect a prodigy, protect a vision. I started to sacrifice my now's for my later's. In other words, I was going to do what I needed to do and handle business to get where I wanted to be.

Now, no person on earth is perfect. We all make mistakes every day, whether knowingly or unintentionally. Both help to shape our futures somehow. What's funny is that our imperfections end up molding us perfectly into who we are supposed to be. If it wasn't for the hard times, good times wouldn't feel so good. The grind and hunger wouldn't be there if everything was easy. I decided I was going to go and get it and use those hard times as fuel to remember why I was going so hard. I tell myself all the time, "I'm coming for it all. I'm coming for everything they said I couldn't have."

You can relate it to getting an ass-whooping. I know, work with me. Whenever I got a whooping from my mom, I would do everything possible not to do the same thing that earned me that ass-whooping in the first place. If you know that something or someone is holding back from following your passion, would you do everything possible to not attract the same toxic things? I've seen and experienced some tough times, and I have mentally prepared myself for the war commonly referred to as the world. I am going to do everything possible to never allow history to repeat itself.

At times, I feel like my life isn't my life anymore but a statement for other young boys and girls to understand that it is possible. "What's possible?" you ask. Anything you want to come true and that's the God honest truth. Sometimes it's like I am no longer living for me. And I'm perfectly fine with that because we all can make it out of our situations, as long as we want to make it out. What's important to remember is that unlike what's always portrayed on TV— the rappers, the fast cars and diamond watches, the Insta-models, the athletes, and many of the random social celeb statuses, that those aren't your only options to call yourself somebody. I see it so much. A lot of young kids are convinced those are the only ways to call themselves successful, the only way they aren't a *nobody* in this world. Well I'll tell you this, don't limit yourself to thinking there is only one way to living comfortably. You can be anything you want- an author, a marketing manager, an entrepreneur, no limit to what could be accomplished. As you read this sentence, slow down on these words right here: *you have a purpose; you are somebody*. You have so much untapped power, and once you realize it, you will begin to accomplish more than you could imagine. As you read this sentence, slow down on these words right here: *nothing is ever out of reach ; you can be and do anything in this life*. Don't allow your mind to become consumed with what the next man or woman is doing. Focus on you and stay the course. Always remember the main goal for what it is you want to accomplish in life, and don't get caught up on the small obstacles that happen in between.

*　　*　　*

I began to walk a different kind of walk. I walked with a different type of confidence. For once, things seemed to somewhat come together for me, only to fall back apart. Around 2006, my mom remarried and soon after I was no longer an only child, they gave birth to a beautiful baby girl. My step-dad Robert worked a lot and was sometimes gone for weeks at a time, so I took on the challenges of helping to take care of the ladies in the house the best I could. This was a great time in life because for once I felt like I had a complete family—the whole TV picture: a mom, dad, son, and daughter look. I'm not gonna flex though. It was awkward sometimes.

I was used to not having a male figure in the house, and for a while, to have one present was weird for me. It was weird calling him "Dad." I almost felt like I was forcing it. But I always appreciated him for stepping in the way he did, much respect. He treated me like his own, and I could imagine how hard it was to try to be a man for another man's kid. Nonetheless, everything seemed together, and I enjoyed the image of our newfound family.

One thing about him was he was huge on laughing and playing pranks. He would always joke around and make us laugh. I remember being sixteen and waking up one Monday morning to go catch the bus to school. I could smell bacon sizzling from my room, so I stopped in the kitchen before walking out the door. He always had a way of using his native Louisiana seasonings to wake up the entire house. Excited to get breakfast, I walked into the kitchen and tapped him on the shoulder before making my way to the refrigerator to pour a cup of orange juice.

I said, "Good morning."

He replied, "Good morning, Son."

I was caught a little off guard because of how he responded to me. His words were slurred and gargled as if he tried to talk with a mouth full of water. I turned around and put my cup on the opposite end of the counter. Not thinking anything of the way he answered, I looked at him and laughed because I knew he enjoyed making jokes. I knew he was joking around as usual, and I thought nothing of it so I continued laughing. I noticed the time on the stove clock. I had five minutes to make it to the bus stop or else I would be making a two-hour walk to school. Scrambling now, I missed breakfast, went to grab my book bag, and said, "See you later, Pops," as I expeditiously moved out the door.

You know, some things that take place early in our lives almost seem like they never happened. I can't remember taking my first steps as a baby. I don't know what my first words were. I can't even remember why I was in such a rush to be an adult. But one thing I will never forget is this moment—the laughs and good times we all shared before my mom's and four-year-old sister's lives would drastically change.

I came home from school later that afternoon, and as I walked into our apartment, I noticed my mom sitting down in the living room. She seemed upset about something, so naturally, as her son, I went to first hug her, and then I asked what was wrong. She opened up about what was bothering her, which turned into a thirty-minute conversation I didn't expect to have right then.

That awkward, funny "Good morning" response Robert gave me earlier that morning wasn't him trying to be funny. All I could think about was how I could've done something different to realize something was wrong. After talking with my mom, she informed me that he had had a seizure the night prior while he was asleep. He stopped breathing for a short period of time but regained consciousness.

After processing this information, I put two and two together. His seizure was the reason for his slurred speech earlier that morning. He wasn't playing around, not this time! He wasn't playing! And that was why he never turned around to look at me directly while we were in the kitchen. He always wanted to be strong and handle things on his own so it made sense why he didn't reach out for help that morning. Was it ego? Nah, I don't think so. Was it pride? No, I don't believe that was it either. He was just being strong. He helped me to understand that any situation I endured was always going to be more mental than anything else. If I ever give up on myself, it will be because I have made my problems bigger than my mindset. He helped me to build that mental toughness, and that's what it is, mental toughness. He knew he would get through this, and that is why he didn't turn to look at me. He wanted to stay strong.

I finally found out that the seizure was only the beginning. I found out that he was experiencing a disease that was eating at his brain, which had caused the previous events to occur. After treatments, after the tears and understanding the effects of what this disease would do long-term, we had to put him in hospice care. At the time, I thought hospice was short for hospitality, which in other words was some type of young old folks' home to get treated for random diseases until you got better. I was informed otherwise. This would be his last stop, the last stop until God was ready to call him home.

Five months later, my mom, sister, and I were home eating and preppin' for school the next day. After we ate dinner, we took our showers and went to bed. It wasn't unusual for me to be up late watching TV on a school night, and this night was no different. Around 10:30 p.m., I was still up watching TV, trying to force myself to go to sleep. I could hear footsteps outside of my door, and the next thing I heard was the knob turning. The door opened, and my heart skipped a beat. I was watching a scary movie, and I thought this shit really came out the TV to get me. You know, the late-night terrors. Plus, I wasn't supposed to be up this late on a school night. Normally, when I heard someone coming, I'd hurry up and turn the TV off and then play sleep until they left. I didn't do that this time. I decided to take the curse out when she walked in and saw the TV still on.

Of course, it was my mom who walked in. I was ready for a showdown, but she didn't start the conversation that way. She stood by the door for a few moments before walking over to my bed. She came over to sit by my foot. I sat up on the bed, thinking that she couldn't sleep either and wanted to kick it with her son for a minute. It was kind of awkward because she didn't say anything initially. She looked at the TV for a few seconds and then looked my way a couple of times before saying anything. After a solid thirty seconds, she opened her mouth and said, "He passed away."

I immediately knew whom and what she was talking about. Speechless. I didn't know what to say, how to react, which emotion to show. Without words, we just embraced each other.

The day of the funeral came. I had never seen my mom like that. I knew that day I had to be a strong presence for her but, more imperatively, for my little sister. She was only four years old. This little girl had just lost the man who had brought her into the world, she loss her daddy. After we walked into the church, it was time to view the body for the last time. I walked up to the casket to see him before it would be closed forever. As I was standing over his body, I picked my little sister up and held her in my arms. I watched her look down at him and then look at me. She said, "When is Dad going to wake up?"

Wow. That still has me messed up a little even putting that there for you to read. Like what the fuck do you say to that? Man, I didn't know how to respond. She's a little kid, man, not really understanding what was going on fully except for seeing people crying and her dad lying in front of her with his eyes closed. Before I could get choked up on my words and emotions, I looked this little girl in the eyes and said, "Tiff…Dad is going away for a while." I inhaled deeply and then continued, "We have to say goodbye."

She looked back down at him and moments later put her face into my shoulder. I walked away shortly after that to our seats. She was right by my side the entire service. To this day, I debate with myself if that was the right thing to tell her right then and there. But I don't know what else I could've said to cushion the loss. With all the emotions built up from being at a funeral alone, I did my best to stay composed. I was on the program to read a verse from the Old Testament. I had to get up in front of all these crying faces to read a scripture from the Bible, and I did, for the most part.

I decided to read Psalm 23:4–6: "Yea, though I walk through the valley of the shadow of death, I will fear no evil: for thou art with me; thy rod and thy staff they comfort me…Surely goodness and mercy shall follow me all the days of my life: and I will dwell in the house of the Lord forever." I didn't shed a tear the entire service. I couldn't. I emotionally could not do it. I couldn't contribute to my mom and little sister crying anymore at seeing me shed tears. So I held back. My main concern was them. It hurt my heart deeply because I understood what that loss would do to my family. I just knew that I had to man the fuck up and be the man presence in the house.

In many instances, I never stopped. Even from a young age, I have always assumed that role. My heart really went to wanting to be that father figure for my little sister. I could never replace her dad, and I understood that. In the same breath, I could love her so much that she understood what real love from a man felt like—the way Robert would've loved her. I could teach her so much about being independent so she wouldn't have to depend on a man for anything. I didn't really know how to be a big brother, and I especially didn't know how to be a father figure. I guessed I was going to get a crash course on both. They needed me more than ever, and I just could not fail.

At the time, I didn't know what the future would hold for my family, but what I did know was that my mom had me, and I had my mom and sister. Why do I share this with you? I know how it feels. I know how it feels to not have a father in the household to raise something he helped bring into the world. I know how it feels to be raised by a single mother. I know how it feels to try to make ends meet when the shit is just so hard. I know how it feels to lose someone close, so close to you. I also know how it feels to feel like a part of you is missing and you can't quite figure out what it is. I share this because you need to know that through it all, you can still make it.

From that day on, it was grind time. I have to make it. I have to! Say it with me: *I have to make it!* No excuses. I have no other choice but to escape the rough start so it doesn't become a rough ending. Accomplishing my goals and ensuring my family, generations to come, are set when I'm long gone are what matters in spite of the pain and hurt. It's bigger than you. You have to make it because your mom needs you. Your sister needs you. You need you. Make it happen.

Miami, Florida 1994 with my orthopedic shoes

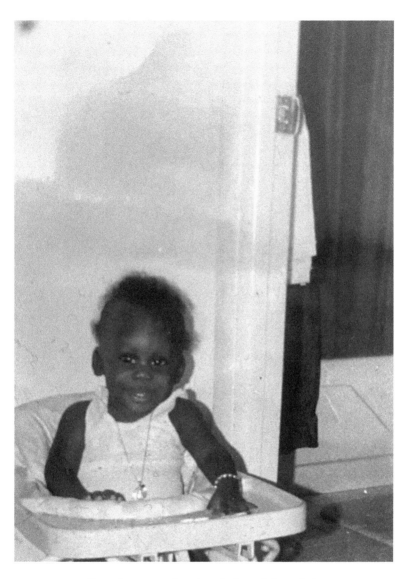

Just the cutest chocolate baby with no hair

Atlanta, Georgia 1999

At a drill meet with Stockbridge High cheering my team on

Beginning of Senior year, I was named cadet battalion commanding officer. My mom and sister in company

Receiving my nomination from Congressman
Scott after delivering my speech

Graduation picture May 2016

Savannah State NROTC physical training, good ol' days

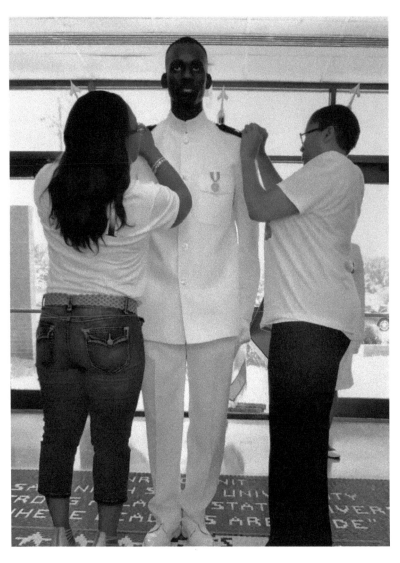

Receiving my commission into the United States Navy July 8, 2016

May 24, 2020 while on deployment, making another entry

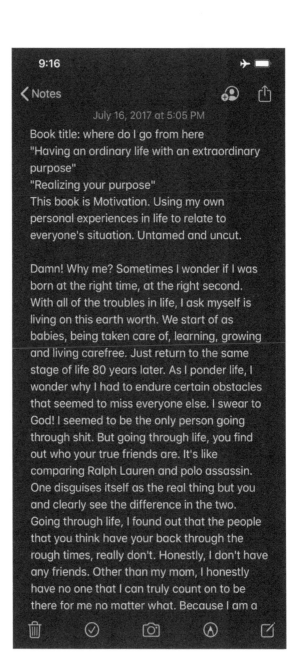

July 16, 2017 at 5:05 PM

Book title: where do I go from here
"Having an ordinary life with an extraordinary purpose"
"Realizing your purpose"
This book is Motivation. Using my own personal experiences in life to relate to everyone's situation. Untamed and uncut.

Damn! Why me? Sometimes I wonder if I was born at the right time, at the right second. With all of the troubles in life, I ask myself is living on this earth worth. We start of as babies, being taken care of, learning, growing and living carefree. Just return to the same stage of life 80 years later. As I ponder life, I wonder why I had to endure certain obstacles that seemed to miss everyone else. I swear to God! I seemed to be the only person going through shit. But going through life, you find out who your true friends are. It's like comparing Ralph Lauren and polo assassin. One disguises itself as the real thing but you and clearly see the difference in the two. Going through life, I found out that the people that you think have your back through the rough times, really don't. Honestly, I don't have any friends. Other than my mom, I honestly have no one that I can truly count on to be there for me no matter what. Because I am a

My first entry made to Where Do I Go from Here

Meeting my daughter for the first time at
three months old, October 5, 2020

CHAPTER 4

NEVER STOP WORKING

I remember staying in this apartment complex on Rex Road in Ellenwood, Georgia for a year. This apartment was actually kind of nice, and I wasn't trippin' too much because I had my own bathroom there. The first few nights after we got our stuff moved in were unusual for some reason. I remember waking up in the mornings and seeing rat droppings all over the living room floor. Ahh, hell nah! The place had rats running through the house at night. I'm frowning up with disgust now as I bring it up. What did my mom and I do about the rats? Well, we couldn't just up and leave the apartment, so we went to the store, bought some rat traps that had this extremely sticky glue on them, and set them up around the house, even in my room. I probably would've passed out if I had woken up to a rat trapped on this sticky pad in my room. Somehow, the rat was supposed to crawl on the sticky pad, and the glue would make the rat immobile.

The next morning in the apartment, one of the rats was in the trap. We caught one in the living room area and my mom made me take it out of the house. *She made me do it.* I was confused on why she couldn't do it, but then she reminded me she was the mama so that was that. I grabbed a plastic bag, picked up the trap with the rat still alive, nervous that the shit would launch out at me, and expeditiously threw it in the bag and sprinted to the dumpster to throw the bag away. This process of catching rats went on for the next eight months we stayed there. It is an uncomfortable and numbing feeling to know you have creatures that don't belong in your house somehow getting in, but again, we did what we had to do. After a while, it became something we adapted to and low-key got use to as bad as it sounds. We really didn't have a choice but to stay there. The rent was cheap and what we could afford.

*   *   *

In high school, I played basketball my ninth-, tenth-, and some of my eleventh-grade year. Why some of my eleventh-grade year? Well, I'll tell you. I transferred to my third high school at the start of my junior year because of some school budget cuts. But even before I get into that part, let me tell you about the undisputedly worst day of my life.

Before the start of my junior year, we had this thing called open house where the kids and parents could come out and see the school, meet teachers, make changes to the kid's class schedule—pretty much ruin your child's life. Well, my mom and I pulled up to the school and stepped foot out of the car. My main mission in getting out of the car was to immediately find the basketball gym because I wanted to see where I would be playing my junior year. If I never believed in destiny before, this day sure enough proved me wrong about what I thought was best for me.

I walked to the front door of the school and noticed after a few jiggles the shit was locked. The entire front side of the building was glass, so I could vividly see the gym from where I was standing. I looked over to my left and noticed another door to this side building connected to the school. My mom and I walked over. I reached for the door, and it was unlocked. As I walked inside this side building, I was walking so fast that I wasn't really paying attention to my surroundings or to what type of building this was. I really didn't care, so I kept walking all the way out the door at the end of the hallway that led to the gym. I looked back to see that my mom wasn't following me anymore, but I could see her standing still. This lady was still inside this side building. I slowed down and turned in her direction to focus my attention on what she was doing. It looked like she was talking to this person dressed in camouflage. Man, I have to be blind right now because I can't really see shit. I walked closer to the door that I had walked out of, and sure enough, she was talking to this short but very muscular gentleman in a brown camouflage uniform. *Ohhhhhhh, shit!* Then it hit me. I looked at the very obvious sign by the door, and it read, "NJROTC Building." Just my luck, bruh. I walked through the damn military building, dawg.

There my mom was, selling my soul to the man right before my eyes. I damn near put my lips and both hands on the glass door saying, "Mama, no, no, no, no, no!"

After another three minutes, she finally walked out of the NJROTC (Naval Junior Reserve Officer Training Corps) Building. She gave me this weird look, and I gave her this weird look back. Confused as to what took her so long to come out, I finally broke the awkward silence and said, "Ma, I am here to play basketball—that's it, damn it." I whispered the "damn it" to myself so she couldn't hear me (that's why the font is smaller). I felt like I had made my point though because she didn't say anything; she just continued to follow me to our ultimate destination—the basketball gym.

It was nice! A tiger was the mascot so it was only fitting that the center of the gym floor had a large tiger on it. There were a lot of seats in the stands, and it was a pretty large open gym. That excited me. I even got a chance to meet the coach for the team, who seemed crazy as hell but cool overall. I couldn't wait to get started there and be a Stockbridge Tiger.

The first day of school came around a couple of weeks later, and I arrived at school. I forgot to print my schedule out beforehand so I went to the main office to get it there. I was all smiles, greeting people, "Have a nice day"-ing people, and shit. Really just excited for the first day and a fresh beginning to play basketball. I walked out of the front office and looked down at my schedule to see where my first couple of classes were. Homeroom was in room 208, and my first-period class was 211, so I was thinking, *Great, not a far walk in the mornings.* I continued to look down the schedule and saw second period was economics, third period was some type of math, fourth period was English, lunch—Thank God!—fifth period....Wait. What the fuck? Oh no. This human being (i.e., my mom) did not do this. There is no way, bro. Fifth period, *NJROTC Building.*

This had to be a joke, but knowing her, I realized this was no laughing matter. I was hot about this, because for one, I had no idea what the fuck JROTC even stood for. Two, I was straight on the whole military act. I just wanted to hoop. But there I was. Fifth period rolled around, and it was day one of *JROTC. Can't wait to see how this goes*, I thought. I walked into the building, ironically the same door that got me into this mess in the first place. The first thing I heard was "Buuuublahhhhhbooooo." It sounded exactly how you just read it, so read that again and say it louder in your head. That was exactly what it sounded like, hearing this kid my age yelling at me. Turns out he wanted me to tuck my shirt in. Well, all you had to do was ask.

I guess that was a rule they had, for males to tuck their shirts in and not wear earrings. Mind you, the school didn't care, but the JROTC program had their own set of rules inside their building. I was thinking to myself, *Yep, this is a bad start already.* Then it dawned on me as I continued walking inside: there were more kids dressed like the kid who yelled "*Buuuublahhhhhbooooo*" earlier. And these kids were decked out in all types of colorful ropes and ribbons and ranks, so I assumed quickly in my head that these were probably the kid leaders or some shit.

All right, I'll play along. As I was tucking my shirt inside my pants, I turned the corner only to meet more kids decked out in colorful ropes and ribbons and ranks, who yelled at me for no reason. There were at least three of them, but I was pretty nonchalant to the voice raising and theatrics. But as I was walking toward the stairs, following the signs that said "Orientation" with an arrow, I glanced over my right shoulder and saw the man responsible for me being in this hellhole: Gunnery Sergeant Stackhouse! Not only were these kids legit screaming at me, I looked in his direction for help, and he gave me the nastiest smirk. My facial expression was probably priceless as the thought, *Muthafucka, what?* bolted through my head. *I know this dude did not just set me up. Yeah, bruh, it's time to get the fuck out of this class.* Once the bell rang, I was the first one out of the building, first to untuck my shirt, and first to make it to my sixth-period class. I couldn't wait for this day to end.

Going home was one of the most awkward times because my great first day of school was overshadowed by one class that I didn't even want to be in from the start. I felt I had been set up, and my mom confirmed it. As I walked into the living room, my mom asked, "How was the ROTC class?" She didn't ask me how my day went, how the bus ride home was, or how lunch tasted. This lady immediately asked me the one thing that was terrible about my day from the jump.

"Well, Mother, I'll tell you," I said as I put my book bag on the ground. "I will be dropping this class tomorrow morning and getting a new elective." I wasn't even sure if I had the power to do that, but I said it anyway.

My mom looked at me and said, "It's only been one day."

I looked at her soul and said, "Well, Mother, it only takes one time to put your hand on a hot stove to not put your hand there anymore. It only takes one time to bite your tongue while you're eating to realize, damn, I need to slow down chewing." I can't remember my next *it only takes one time* example, but she got the point after the first one. Even after I had stated a strong case, she convinced me to stay in at least a week to get a full opinion on the program before calling it quits, and I agreed. I did. I gave it a try, being open-minded. I went back the next day and the days after that. About a month into the program, I got the opportunity to lead different groups and realized people listened to me. I wasn't sure if this was a plan to allow me to realize my potential or to unlock this raw talent and personality in a different aspect, but I didn't look at it like that. I was just being myself. I would do JROTC during the day and basketball early in the mornings when we had practice and after school when we had practice, meetings, or games. My mom supported me doing both, but as the season went on, the games got tougher, the practices got longer, and my energy reflected in the classroom. Basketball demanded a lot of me, and I wasn't producing on the court. JROTC became demanding because I was now responsible for numerous teams, such as the drill team, the color guard team, and the physical training team, all in preparation for drill meets we competed in with other high schools in our district. It was too much for me to handle. It wasn't from a stress standpoint because I never bitched or complained about anything. In my mind, I could do any- and everything. *I can take on the world—I'm Superman.* But one thing I prided myself most on started to slip in all three aspects, and that was my performance. Being that I couldn't drop school, I knew I needed to let basketball or JROTC go. Both deserved the proper attention and quality that I couldn't give anymore. So, I let one go.

The decision to pursue one over the other was hard. I loved basketball and knew I could make it somewhere overseas if I really worked and trained. I loved JROTC, as odd as that was for me to accept. I had tapped into a new version of myself and displayed things I never thought I could do.

I put my big boy pants on and made a decision to leave one, essentially forever. I laid out my options and thought about which aspect I could truly excel in and thrive in long-term. I had switched schools to play basketball and set myself for options after high school. Two months into my junior year, I found myself making a big-time decision that was going to shape the rest of my life. So the decision was clear for me. I made it, and I didn't look back.

* * *

Senior year of high school! There I was, arguably in the best and most important year of grade school. So many decisions I needed to make, like "What am I gonna do with my life after this year? Which college will I go to? Shit, will I even go to college? If I do, what will I get my degree in? When do I start applying? Wait. How will I pay for school? I heard it's not cheap. I definitely don't have a college fund or money stashed somewhere for this. That college fund I did have we had to use for gas on pump three. [Insert laugh] I love you,

Ma. And lastly, what would be my final impression I'd leave on my high school?"

I had a lot of questions going into my senior year of high school, and I could not answer any of them. I knew myself to be a decent person. I had mediocre grades and the gift of personality but had ten months to essentially plan the rest of my life. No matter what I was going to do, my plans did not include being home. It was time to move forward and move out into the world on my own. Stepping into adulthood is a tremendously frightening leap, and I had no idea where to start.

At the beginning of senior year, I was announced as the battalion commanding officer of my NJROTC unit. I couldn't believe that people really believed in me to take charge of anything, especially considering I had only been at the school for one full year before transferring from my last school. Who knew that the path I truly believed I was traveling was designed for this one moment, this one chance? See, that is how God works. Right then and there, he knew that July 2010 I would be introduced to my true purpose. Then and there, it happened. Cadet Butler reporting for duty.

Senior year was my reality check. After ninth grade, you know you have tenth grade and then eleventh grade. But after twelfth grade, there is no thirteenth grade. Real life is next, and there is no class or course that can really prepare you for it. Somehow, you just figure it out as much as you can and prepare as best as possible. Being a part of the JROTC military program presented different opportunities after high school. Whether it was entering the Navy or Army as an E-3 vice E-1 because I had the program under my belt or going to college, I had the increased tools to be a productive young African American man in the real world. The road wasn't smooth though.

My instructors in the program talked to me about the benefits of going to school and having it paid for by the navy. Ehhhhh, sounded too good to be true. They explained to me how the military would pay for my tuition. Essentially, I would be receiving a free education. Sounds good, but my tenth-grade economics taught me "T-I-N-S-T-A-A-F-L" (Translation: There Is No Such Thing as a Free Lunch). So what did I have to do in return for the Navy? That was my follow-up question because I could only imagine that serving in the United States Navy and participating in the Stockbridge High School NJROTC program had different requirements. I thought about that conversation for a couple of days.

Not knowing what I would be getting myself into exactly, I started applying for Navy scholarships. I'm all about having options, and I didn't want to starve myself of a potentially good opportunity so I made the process happen. I remember it like it was yesterday. The first scholarship I ever applied to was a Navy scholarship called the Alternative Scholarship Reservation (ASR). With a lot of scholarships, your GPA had to be really good to be competitive. Plus, there were only a handful of these scholarships offered at the time, so this was really competitive.

Now I wasn't lazy or anything in school, but I wholeheartedly believed my GPA wasn't a true reflection of how smart I was! It didn't matter what I thought, because I looked mediocre on paper. I understood my chances and knew what I was up against. I got everything I needed, including recommendation letters. I had written my personal statement and was ready to submit my application for the ASR. I got a response within three weeks of submitting my application. I was denied. It sucked being told no because I took that as "We don't want you." I trained myself to understand just because a door slams on you doesn't mean that was the only way inside the house. So I didn't stop. I immediately went on the internet to search for other scholarship opportunities and ran across the National ROTC Scholarship. I applied for it quick; the deadline was three days away so I guess I caught it just in time. It took me probably a day or two to get everything together to submit my application. I sent it off and saw my response a few weeks later. I was denied.

At this point, I felt that I was shooting a three-pointer in a dark gym. My chance at making the shot was extremely slim, so I switched gears. I gave up on that Navy option and started putting effort into college programs. At the same time, I still didn't have the money to pay for anything after high school, so I was back to square one. I was overwhelmed that life was around the corner, and I was not prepared. So I threw my hands up and decided that I was going to figure out my life when the time was right. I couldn't help but feel like nothing was going my way, and after being denied multiple times for a scholarship, giving up was the next option for me. I know what I said about there being another way inside the house, but maybe I was trying to get into the wrong house.

This caused me to refocus and get right. I wasn't sure of the outcome anymore, but I knew if I was going to stop, then it would be after I'd given it all I had. So not just yet, I had one more shot to give this. I'm not just telling you a story about how I got denied and how much it sucked. I'm giving you tools. Think about it and reread this chapter if need be.

Rewind back to senior year as I attempted to put the pieces of my future together. One distinct memory I have is applying to attend a service academy, and it was a very dynamic process, from collecting various documents and recommendation letters to recording how far I could throw a basketball. In addition, one of the requirements was to obtain a congressional nomination from a local congressman. Well, great! I'm damn sure not getting in because I do not know anyone who would even come close to writing me a nomination. I tried anyway.

After being low-spirited because of being denied scholarships and colleges previously, I was starting to come to terms with the idea that this probably wasn't for me. I reached out anyway, kind of on my last attempt to try this college thing. I wrote a sincere letter to a local congressman named Mr. David Scott, in my desire to receive his recommendation to attend the service academy. Honestly, I was not expecting a response let alone a yes, but he wrote me back. He really wrote me back. I received his response stating that he would be honored to nominate me. I immediately dropped and fell to tears. At this point, my determination bypassed military reasons. I was now geared to showing that even if a million people tell you no, you keep going until you get that one yes.

The day arrived when I received my nomination from the congressman personally in ceremony fashion. I can remember being overwhelmed with so many emotions that day. There were other recipients there to accept their nominations into various service academies like the Air Force Academy, West Point, and the Naval Academy. I can remember feeling that I didn't belong there, like I wasn't good enough to be among those other high school kids who seemed to be way more prepared than I was—prepared for life, prepared for the military and everything that came with it. I felt as if I were in line to get on a ride at the amusement park, ready and pumped to start the ride. And then I got to the front of the line ready to get on and they stopped entry because they'd boarded everyone the ride could hold. Despite my feelings, there I was, ready to conquer one of the most immense moments of my life. No going back now.

Prior to the ceremony starting, all the recipients sat in the first few rows in preparation to walk center stage to receive their congressional nomination from the Congressman Scott. I was the fifth or sixth kid in the lineup. Just like with any award you receive, it's customary to give a speech or offer quick words expressing gratitude. I recall listening to the first couple of speeches, and I remember thinking to myself, *Dang! This sounds really professional and rehearsed.* Needless to say, I did not prepare a thing. It really wasn't even on my mind to prep something to say beforehand because I had no idea how this worked. I had no speech, and as the line to receive nominations dwindled down and it was closer to me going up, I not only drew blanks on what I could possibly say in a room filled with hundreds of people, but I also forgot my own damn name before getting up there.

My nerves set in. After a while, it was finally my time to walk center stage and accept my nomination. As I was making this walk, I started to remind myself why I was there. I was in this position in my life to show something, to prove something. I don't prepare speeches. That has never been in my nature because my authenticity comes from feeling the moment and letting my heart speak for me. In other words, what got me there was staying true to myself, and I wasn't going to change that now.

I was front and center. The congressman presented the award to me and handed me the microphone and floor to speak. I let my heart talk. Once I finished speaking, the room was in tears. I gave one of the most heartfelt speeches I hadn't prepared for. I simply spoke about my life, my struggle. I invited the audience to listen to a quick three-minute glimpse of my life and what it took to get there. To have my mom sitting in the crowd reminiscing and looking at me so proudly added to my emotions while I was talking. I had a story to tell.

When I got the microphone, I wanted people to understand that I took a bunch of left turns before I finally got one right. People were going to understand that this was real, true pain and that I was there because God scripted this for my family and me. If they didn't remember anything else from my speech, my name, or how I looked years from then, I wanted them to remember these words: "Don't ever question how you made it here; just be ready to show the world why you belong." That day, I did just that, and I decided I would always stay true to myself.

A couple of months after the ceremony, I had everything I needed to send off a strong package as a candidate into the Naval Academy. Now it was time to wait for a response to see if I was accepted. I remember going to check the mail at least three times a week, hoping it had come. I received nothing in the mail for another month. Then, finally, on a Thursday evening, I saw mail from Annapolis, Maryland, and knew this was it. I couldn't even wait for my mom to get home to open it, so I opened the mail on the walk home.

As I opened it, the first two words I saw were "Thank you." I continued reading to discover that I had not been accepted. Now, with this news, my thought process went multiple ways. *Damn! Am I not good enough?* You start to feel that way when you've been denied so many times. It's like if you are really good at a sport and one of the top schools doesn't want to take you, it could make you question your own confidence in yourself. But I quickly snapped out of that feeling because I had to be thankful for making it there and even being blessed with the opportunity to do something different and positive. I made up my mind right then and there that I was not going to stop. And I didn't.

With all of the trials and misfortunes occurring my senior year of high school, I cannot dismiss all of the good that year brought me. I cried, but on the opposite end, I smiled. I was nearing the end of my high school career, and it was time to make decisions. I can remember talking with my mom about different options after graduation, but college never really appeared realistic to me. Really, me? College? Come on now. I was a decently smart guy, but my grades weren't that notable, so there went my chance of an academic scholarship. I had stopped playing basketball, so there went my chance at getting an athletic scholarship. My mom made it clear to me that I was either going into the military or going to college after high school. One option seemed more realistic than the other. So I began to talk to recruiters and make slight preparations to enlist. I took the SAT and ACT just to give the college idea a try, but my scores were so low that I knew I couldn't compete for a spot in someone's college. Actually, my scores were so low that the SAT results told me I wasn't ready for college. And my 16 on the ACT furthered proved I wasn't going to college, not with them low ass scores.

One of my instructors told me about another military scholarship that was out there and that I should apply for. It made sense; I was already involved in the JROTC program in high school. I can remember putting my name on three different navy scholarship applications and being rejected all three times. All the signs led to me counting myself out, even though I knew I had what it took to be successful in any avenue I wanted to pursue. It seemed like giving up was never a choice I had though. It was either make it happen or make it happen by any means necessary. With my low-ass test scores, I knew I would get counted out on paper, but I knew I had the mental toughness and mind-set to be as great as the next man. I applied to two historically black college and university (HBCU) institutions—not because I was pro-Black or because my family had a tradition of attending predominantly black schools or anything but because they would give me a chance—a chance to pursue a degree, a chance that predominantly white institutions (PWIs) wouldn't give me.

In the fall of 2011, I began to receive letters from the two colleges I applied to. The first letter I received, I was so hyped! All my hard work and dreams were finally falling into place. Someone was going to see the work I put in and allow me to excel at their institution. I waited on my mom to come home from work to open it because I wanted her to witness the great news. She finally came home, and we sat down, both filled with emotions as I began to open the letter. You know how you anticipate something so much that you don't read everything all the way? You just skim over it to look for the apparent good words?

Well, I opened the letter, and the first word I saw was "Unfortunately." My heart sank, and so did my mom's, but ironically, I didn't hang my head down. I can still remember that instant feeling. It was a feeling of anger and motivation mixed. Weird combination, right? It's simple: when you believe in a plan that someone higher than you has designed for you, things start to stress you less and you begin to trust more. I stood up and hugged my mom because I knew it was going to be all right in the long run.

A few weeks later, I got another letter in the mail from the other college I applied to. This time, I didn't wait for my mom to get home to open it because in a sense, if I was denied again, I didn't want her to be disappointed in me. My plan was to open it and then throw it away if it was another rejection letter so I could move on. I opened the letter and simultaneously took a drink of water. As I skimmed over the letter, the first word I noticed read "Congratulations!" Not knowing how to feel, I immediately tried to play it off to myself like "Yeah, I just got accepted into college. It's whatever." That lasted maybe ten seconds, and then I called my mom. As I put the phone to my ear, she walked in, and I shouted something weird while waving the acceptance letter in my hand.

Right then, I knew the work had only begun. I had been accepted into an HBCU, and that was the best news of my life! But I had no way to pay for it still. Fuck! My family didn't have tuition, housing, books, and fees money just lying around, so I understood getting accepted was 1 percent of the battle; financing it was the other 99 percent. When I think about it, opportunities come to three types of people: people who get through because of who they know and/or who knows them, people who are at the right place at the right time, and the rest of the world who create their own opportunities by any means. I realized which category I fell into the tough way.

This next event that occurred, I was definitely two of those three. Early on, I developed the understanding that I had to be great to even be considered—not good, but great. Well, guess what. I had to make it no matter what.

One early morning, a gentleman who ran the college navy ROTC program a few hours from the school I had just gotten accepted into came down to do an inspection of the JROTC program I was battalion commander of.

I remember the short gentleman arriving at the school, coming up to me, and saying, "Let's see how this goes."

Well, all right, I guess. With me being the battalion commander over the one hundred plus cadets, I had to make sure we did well, or it would look bad on the program, the school, and me. Fast-forward, we passed the inspection with flying colors. Now, remember when I said in the next event that would occur, I was two of those three people? This was that opportunity, that rare chance you have to grab or else you miss. I created my own opportunity by working extremely hard, and I was in the right place at the right time. God had this planned for me all along.

After the inspection, the captain who was in charge of the college NROTC program sat me down, and we had a two-minute conversation about what he observed at the school. Then he asked me questions about where I was from, about my family, about my financial state in regards to college, and about what I wanted to do with my life. The next sentence that came from his mouth would change my life forever. I answered the question about my plans for the future.

One of the things I can recall saying is that "I just want to be successful in everything I do and be able to take care of my mom and little sister."

He then said, "Well, I'll tell you what. I am going to offer you a scholarship to my NROTC program, paid tuition so you can get your degree, and a commission into the United States Navy."

How did I respond? I responded like any poised eighteen-year-old kid would. I fainted. It was a very quick faint though. You could barely tell, but I for sure drifted off into La-La Land.

Once I came back to my senses, before he could change his mind for some reason or realize that I had fainted and say, "Uhmmmmm, you know what? Never mind, bruh," I said, "Sir, thank you. I am ready to work!"

*   *   *

Before leaving for college, I really didn't realize the extent of the opportunities that lay ahead. At the same time, I did understand I had busted my ass to make those opportunities come my way, but I guess a part of me didn't conceptualize the full meaning behind everything that was getting ready to take place. I had a mentor in high school, Mr. Thaxter Kelley, who would always go out of his way to make sure I kept focus on important things like school and plans for the future. He did that even before I got a scholarship or accepted to anybody's college. So you could imagine when I did secure the opportunity for both options how proud of me he was. Here and there, we would go and sit down at a restaurant to break bread, and Mr. Thaxter would counsel me about life. I always enjoyed those times, and I always got something out of each meeting we had.

One time in particular, this was about two weeks before I was leaving for college to start the NROTC program, he called me and asked, "Hey, Torrey, you ready for your future?"

I responded, "Yes, sir, as ready as I am going to be."

The conversation rounded off with us setting up another mentoring session over food the following day. We decided to meet at the Truett's on Mt. Zion Road to break bread and discuss life. That day changed the way I would think for the rest of my life. As we were sitting down talking, he began to open up to me, sharing his personal college experiences and how being an Omega man and playing football had shaped his life.

Throughout everything he said, these were the words that stood out to me. He said to me, "Never forget why you are there." I quote that same phrase to this day. But to make it hit home a bit more, he asked me a series of questions. The first question he asked me was "Why do you go to a restaurant?"

OK, weird question to ask, but I played along. I answered with the obvious response: "To eat of course."

Then he asked me, "Why are you going to school now?"

At this point, I was over the senseless questions and was ready for the point in all of this. Plus, I was hungry, so I was impatiently waiting on my food to come out while being interrogated. I answered his question with another obvious response: "To get an education."

His last question was "Now, why are you going to college?"

I thought about it a few seconds before I answered. I responded with "To get my degree."

Mr. Thaxter excitedly said, "Exactly!" with a higher-pitched tone in his voice. He began to break down the reason for each question.

"You see, you go to a restaurant to eat, point-blank. You may get a little entertainment with music while you wait or a glass of water. All of that is cool in the meantime, but the main purpose of going to the restaurant is to eat." He went on to explain the purpose of me being in school, and the same principles applied. Mr. Thaxter continued, "Now, when I asked you why you are going to college, you told me to get your degree, right?"

I nodded my head yes.

He explained to me that going to college is one of the best experiences anyone can get. I mean, let's be real, the partying, staying out late, exploring, becoming your own person—it's a great time. My face lit up when he said the partying part, so it was hard to focus on anything else after that. But he paused for a second and said, "Here is what you need to remember."

At this point, I was not focused on anything else but speeding up these two weeks so I could get on the ladies. He could tell I wasn't really focusing anymore so he told me to listen very closely to what he was going to say next. I leaned forward and tuned in. Once he noticed my attention was there, he went on to explain that going to a restaurant was the exact same as my reasoning for going to college. He said, "Once you get to college, there are going to be a lot of organizations you can participate in, a lot of drugs and temptations, a lot of girls, and a lot of sex will be offered to you. While that is fine and well, all of that is the music being played at the restaurant. It's cool in the meantime, while you wait."

Everything he said earlier all came together. I was going to see and experience things while I was there, but if my goal was to get my degree, then that was the reason for going, and everything else that happened within those four years was "in the meantime" on my way to getting that degree. In the grand scheme of things, if you set your mind on achieving something, do not allow the distractions along the way to become your new goal or purpose. I think a lot of times we have a goal in mind when attempting to accomplish something, but we allow the small pleasures along the way to tamper with the reason we set out on the journey to begin with. Don't let it happen. If it's school you want to do, study hard and get that education. If it's sports you are set on, put the training hours in, and be the best you can be. If it's entrepreneurship you want to pursue, start getting your business portfolio together and devising a plan on how to get your product out there. Whatever the goal is, allow the process to drive you to that end state so you can say these three words when you arrive: "I made it."

The general understanding from this story is never forget why you started. Never forget why you are there. Right there, I set the bar and streamlined what my goal was. Saying "To get an education" in my mind didn't mean I would finish. I could've said "to experience college life" or "to join organizations," but that didn't finish school to me. I was going to college not only to educate myself but to accomplish something I never would have even thought was possible growing up. Trust the process.

Through it all, no one makes it by him- or herself. We all need someone to support us even if it's the one yes we need to make it through the door. Nothing compares to that feeling you get when things are going better than expected. It's almost surreal. If nothing else, I want you to understand that you have the ability to change the world. None of us are born really understanding our true potential until it's seen by others. Those are the people you need to surround yourself with, folks who see what you are and push you to what you could be.

Thank you to those who believed it was possible before it was actually possible—great African American pioneers, such as General Colin Powell, Dr. Martin Luther King Jr., Jack Johnson (the first black boxer to be world heavyweight champion), Rebecca Lee Crumpler (first African American female doctor), Admiral Samuel Gravely, the Golden Thirteen, Doris Miller, and William B. Pinckney just to name a few. Thank you to the everyday people who continue to break barriers unrecognized. Well, I have news for you: you are noticed, and the obstacles you conquer each day are not going unnoticed anymore. You don't have to wear a cape to be a hero; you just have to be worth following. Thank you!

CHAPTER 5

A COUPLE DIFFERENT OPTIONS

College was the start of something that I'd carry with me for the rest of my life. I set out to find myself, learn, and, most important, turn the hell up.

I can remember my mom dropping me off at my dorm. We got out of the car. I looked around, and I couldn't help but notice that there were so many beautiful women walking around. Mack Daddy mode activated. I knew I was going to enjoy Mack Daddy mode being activated. I knew I was going to enjoy myself.

My mom and I walked up to my dorm that would be my new home for freshman year, a nice but small 150-square-foot room with a white wall thrown in the middle of the room which divided my bed from my roommate's. My mom was so embarrassing. For one, she had on a shirt that said, "My son is in college" with a "College Mom" hat to match. To complete the package, my little sister had something similar on. My mom kept emphasizing on the way back downstairs to the car how proud she was of me. This whole college thing was an experience for both of us. As we walked, her words went in one ear and out the other because I could not get over the fact that my mom wore this shirt with the hat to match. I had officially accomplished the most freshman thing I could possibly do, and it hadn't even been a full day. Whatever, although embarrassed, a part of me was like, "Yeah! My family reppin' the kid hard."

They drove off crying and waving goodbye in the car, and I waved back. Once the car was out of sight, I turned toward my dorm building and knew it was time to make it happen on my own—no Mom to wake me up in the morning, no one to tell me when to eat or what to do. I had to be the man I claimed to be, and that meant financially too.

Halfway through the semester, everything was going great. Grades were good, I was doing pretty well in NROTC, and I had finally started making new friends.

One night, I came back to my room from my night class pretty upset. While in class, the professor had called out the names of students whose classes were endanger of being dropped because of unpaid balances owed to the university. My name was among them. Once I got to my room, I went and checked my account to see what the confusion was because I knew there had been a mistake somewhere.

As I looked at the expenses for tuition, room/board, and so on, I came across the total unpaid balance, $1,000. I had a week to come up with a grand, or all my classes would be dropped. And then what? I had no idea. I was thinking to myself, considering all of my options to come up with the money. One option was to get a job that paid roughly one hundred forty-three dollars a day for the next week. Well, there was a strip club down the street from school. I quickly scratched that option off the list for obvious reasons. I thought about every option possible, but none of them were going to get me what I needed in a week in order to stay in school. I did not want to drop out, but as the days got closer to the money being due, I had no money, and I was fresh out of ideas.

Two days out, I finally decided to call my mom and tell her the situation I was in. Around 8:00 p.m., I gave my mom a call. She answered with a sleepy tone and said, "What's up, Son?"

I said, "Ma, I may be coming home earlier than expected."

She asked me what I was talking about. I paused for a second. Eventually, I came out and told her the situation. "Ma, I have a balance of one thousand dollars on my account so my classes are going to be dropped in two days if it is not paid."

Before I could finish rambling about how sorry I was for not having the money to cover my schooling, she said that she would call me back. This was odd. We never hung up the phone abruptly with each other or even without saying, "I love you." It was unusual, and I prayed that I didn't raise her blood pressure stressing her with my issue. Phone connectivity was shitty inside my dorm room, so I waited outside for forty-five minutes, and she still hadn't called back. She had to wake up early in the morning for class, so I figured she had gone to sleep.

I had to wake up early the next morning as well, so I decided to go back inside and call her back in the morning. I felt terrible, disappointed, and upset with myself that my college career was coming to an end because I didn't have the money to cover all of my expenses. I shed a few tears walking back to my dorm. Once I got back to the room, I went toward my laptop to move it off the bed to my desk so I could lie down.

Just before I shut the computer off, I noticed the page that displayed my account balance had timed out. I logged back in to check one more thing before calling it a night. After refreshing the page, I looked and realized my account balance had gone from $1,000 to zero. Confused as shit, I thought, *There is no way in hell this just happened.* Someone with the same name had to have had the same thousand-dollar balance, and when he attempted to pay his balance, mistakenly paid mine. It just didn't make sense to me at all. I rushed outside and tried to call my mom back. She answered after the second try.

She picked up and said in a monotone voice, "Hello." "Hello???""

I ignored that awkward-ass greeting and said, "Hey, Ma, I—" she cut me off and said, "It is taken care of, baby boy. You are never in this alone. Now go get some sleep." She said, "I love you," and I repeated it back before we ended the call.

My mom believed in me. Initially I didn't want to call my family to begin with. It's like knowing who your true friends are. The only family I had to call was Mom, and I knew she did not have that type of money just lying around, especially after paying bills for the month. I didn't want to put that burden and worry on her. But there she was again, Mama making sure I stayed on the course to accomplishing something. I realized being in college was bigger than I was. This was about the village. If I made it, she made it as a single parent. She was just as invested in my education and made sure that it didn't stop when I left home. Mom was still dependable and had my back no matter the cost, literally. I have to make it. I have to.

Others will never really understand your grind because they never walked where you've stepped foot. The goal is the same for everyone wanting to make it, but the grind is different, the reason why is different. I have a mom who dedicated her entire life to making sure I had the tools I needed to build a kingdom. So you know what? I would grind. I decided that I would make sure her sacrifices would not be overlooked, and I was going to make something out of the long, stressful nights.

* * *

In a world that glorifies the negative, it's hard to keep positive energy and consistently do the right things—so many temptations, so many obstacles, but you have to ask yourself, "What keeps me going?" What keeps you focused and locked in on what you need to accomplish? A lot of the time, I questioned my ability to believe in myself and what I brought to the table. You know, most of us have a plan to get out of our current situations in life. We swear up and down that the way we are used to living won't last long. Having a plan is great; at least then you've put thought into the idea, but that's only step one. Take this for thought: You have to plan to get to class on time. You plan to take the ACT and get accepted into college, where you plan to get a degree, and then you plan to get a job afterward. Let's elevate that way of thinking. I had to train my mind to stop planning things. The word *plan* is just a promoted word to say "probably." You have to stop "planning" and start "executing." Instead of saying, "I plan to go to college," "I plan to accomplish this and that," switch up the thought process and say, "I will attend college, but first I will take the ACT, March 29, at the 8:30 a.m. session. Once I receive my test scores in roughly four weeks, I will use those scores to assist in applying for various academic scholarships. During my time in college, I not only want to enjoy the campus student life, parties and all, but I understand those pleasures are temporary. I will set my future up completing and participating in different internships to accommodate my résumé, which will make me more marketable to employers."

Now who sounds like they have their stuff together? The "I plan" person or the "I will" individual? I know who I am placing bets on to actually follow through with the plan. This is your life. You get one first impression. A plan is only as good as a dream; execution is only as good as the plan. Every day is a blessing, and you have to be grateful for everything. The same thing you are complaining about being a problem is the very thing someone in this world is praying for. Just remember, it could always be worse, so smile. I learned that you can't get stressed over things that are not in your control. A lot of people ask me why I am so optimistic, so positive and calm, especially in seemingly stressful situations. It's simple; I don't allow the situations that life brings to get me out of character. I'll put it into simple mathematics: if someone, something, or whatever is adding unnecessary complications to your life, then subtract that variable from the equation. I have a family I have to be there for, and they need me at my best. Who are you here for? What's your motivation? And to answer, at times, you have to reach deep within yourself. Sometimes you are not going to have anyone in your corner clapping for you. It gets really lonely when you walk a path everyone doesn't have directions to, and I am here to let you know it is OK. It is all right. You are holding hands with someone who can reveal more than imaginable blessings. I hold hands with that same individual every day, and he has not led me into danger. Trust him, then trust yourself, and everything will work itself out.

* * *

All of the life experiences that I share represent something in your own personal life. I would say giving up is probably the worst decision anyone can make. The main reason is because it's the easiest decision to make. Just because something starts to get a little challenging and the days become weeks, the weeks become years, is no reason to stop going after what you want. Never forget why you started.

Early on, I learned to take responsibility for my own choices and actions. Blaming other people for the whys in your life does nothing but hold you back from owning your life. The less you take ownership of your life and the more you blame others for what your life isn't or can't be, the less time you have to make your life what it is and what it could be.

*   *   *

The college experience was wide open for me to do anything I wanted. I remember making a few friends within the first couple of months of my freshman year. When I say we did everything together, I mean, when you saw me, it was almost always in the company of my friends. We partied together, hooped together, ate together. The only thing we didn't do together was study— obviously, right? It was college.

Now that I mention partying, I can recall going to some parties freshman year. I guess I can only remember some parties because I was lit for more than half of them. Like how the saying goes, if you remember the party, then you didn't party. Well, that's a fucked-up phrase, but stay with me. Most of the ones I went to were fraternity parties, and man, they were piped [Inject: piped = fun]. This was my first real party experience, specifically in the mix of other people who were young and black. I see how the party lifestyle can become addictive because I couldn't get enough of it that year.

The college campus was surrounded by low-maintenance areas and Section Eight housing. So with that, needless to say, the locals always popped up on camp days and nights. Most of the events held by the university were open to the public so it wasn't usual to see strangers.

It was Friday night, and I had just gotten out of my last class for the day. It was time to unwind after a long week. That was pretty much the end of every week. But this Friday was different for some reason. My friends and I decided to hit up this frat party later that night. The venue was down the street from camp, so we didn't need an Uber or anything, just our two feet. With any good college night, we couldn't just show up to a party without being ready to have a good time. That goes without saying, right? But this meant pregaming. This was the first time in my life I'd ever heard of this.

I learned quickly that college nights had four phases. Phase I was the go home, shower, and get dressed stage. The fit of the night was important, and if I didn't have one that would kill 'em that night, the mall was the first destination. After getting an outfit ready, ironed to get the wrinkles out but not to where my shit had creases in it, I laid it out on the bed, and it was time to take a shower—not just any shower, but the type of shower to make sure my ass was smelling good; you never knew how the night could go. I would brush my teeth like a dude with waves would brush his hair before stepping out.

After a steaming shower, it was time to get dressed but of course not without music. No, no, no. Phase I was essentially a mood starter to prep the mind, body, and soul for a great night. Phase I complete. Now, phase II was the pregame stage where you would link up with the friends you planned to go out with and consume drinks. In other words, it was during this phase you'd get fired up. Lit. Taking shots. Tipsy. Ready to show yo ass. Arguably, depending on the night, the pregame phase is the most important part of the night, and sometimes, it is the best part of the night. It's just you and your friends drinking, laughing, and clowning on each other.

If a party started 8:30 p.m., it was customary to show up at 10:30 p.m. No one showed up to a party on time. The cool playas arrived about two hours late to a party, just in time for the twerking music to pop off. Now on to phase III, the party—the climax of the night and the reason for phases I and II. The party was the time to be dressed fresh as fuck and be lit so you could be loosened up, really to increase your confidence so you could talk to that girl in the third row of class you were scared to holla at on a regular day. With your friends and a couple of drinks in the system, mixed with the fly outfit you put together, it made for a great night to get phone numbers and make moves.

Now, phase IV was definitely the young people phase, only. Phase IV was the after-party phase. A lot of parties in Savannah ended around 2:00 a.m., which in older people time, is too late anyway. In college student time, 2:00 a.m. marks the beginning of the night for some reason. When the parties or clubs shut down, no problem, because during the actual party, guys would promote their "after party" move, whether it was a house party at someone's small-ass apartment or a kickback on camp, which routinely would get shutdown by campus police.

Whatever the move was, we couldn't just go back to our rooms, not on a Friday, Saturday night. It was too early, especially if you didn't get to make your move on a certain young lady. This was another opportunity to shoot that shot to a young lady you let slip away during the party.

Now that all four phases have been explained, back to this particular night. This was my first party of the year, first frat party ever, and I couldn't wait to experience it. I really didn't know what to expect, but I guess that was the advantage. No expectations, except only to have a good time. Phase III was in full effect. My buddies and I met up after getting dressed and chipped in to get a few bottles to get us right. Now, I wasn't a hard drinker at all, so I would get my own personal stash of fruity drinks to pregame with. I would get clowned all the time.

While they were throwing back shots of Henny and all kinds of strong shit, I was throwing back margaritas, yelling, "Cheers, nigga!" Whatever, the fruity drinks made me feel good. In other words, they got the job done by getting me exactly where I needed to be. That is the ultimate goal anyway. Now if you recall from phase III, you didn't show up to a college party on time. This party in particular started at 9:00 p.m., so what time did we leave the spot? About 11:00 p.m. Plus we were on foot, making a twenty-minute walk to the venue. So we were about two and a half hours late to the party. It doesn't make sense to be late at all, but it did in college. Plus, we were feeling ourselves and were ready to get digits that night.

We eventually started our walk to the party, finally making it off camp. We took a side gate that led off camp. The lighting wasn't that good at all, and there wasn't another human being in sight, so this adventure was dangerous already. This was a straight line to the party, so we figured we'd take this way. By this time, it was late in the night and dark outside, so this wasn't the safest thing we could do, especially considering the area that surrounded camp, which wasn't mansions and castles. But who cared? We were young and invincible.

As we walked down the street with poor lighting shining on us about every fifty steps, we were cracking jokes on each other and laughing loudly in somewhat of a disorderly fashion. I could imagine that in some of the housing and apartments we passed, people inside were probably sleeping or resting peacefully on this Friday night. And there we came, walking down the street, making all this damn noise. Off into the distance, we could see a lighted place and faintly hear music from that direction, so I knew we were close to the party. We walked the middle of the road. To the left was an extremely long fence going down the road, and to the right was all housing and apartments along the road. I was walking furthest to the right, closer to the homes.

I decided to look over my shoulders to keep awareness of our surroundings here and there, 'cause these niggas were definitely not concerned about safety. I checked over my right shoulder and noticed three or four guys, locals from the city, standing outside, nearly thirty feet from where I was walking. They were fully dressed, standing up, smoking weed in a semicircle, and kicking it among each other. Shit really didn't strike me as anything unusual, just a couple Black folks kickin' it this Friday night. I turned back to the other side my friends were on, and they didn't notice the group of guys on our right. Of course, they were too busy laughing loud as fuck, and I was assuming the liquor had kicked in because these muthafuckas couldn't walk straight.

For some reason, I sobered up quickly because something didn't feel right. After watching them having a grand time, I looked back over to where I saw the locals and didn't see them anymore. They had left. I completely turned around to see them now walking about twenty yards behind us. I clearly saw that there were four of them. There were four of us. Maybe they were headed to the party too because again, mostly everything was open to the public. They looked rough as hell, but I didn't think too much into it. Now, I started pep-talking myself for the worst-case scenario, where they would start a fight with us.

At this point, I had enough margaritas in my system that I felt I could take on a silverback gorilla, so you couldn't tell me anything. My friends finally noticed the four locals behind us, and, of fucking course, without any hesitation, they started to talk shit about them. Typical, no matter the situation, roasting someone was always the answer for them.

We continued walking, and at that point, we were closer to the party because the music became more apparent. All of a sudden, out of nowhere, the next noise I heard was "Pow, pow, pow!" *Immediately*, with no questions asked or will to figure out who, what, how, and why, we took off running. I ran so fast I ended up running by myself. It's funny how Black people respond to running. If one person runs or even makes the gesture to take off, everybody follows suit with no questions asked until the end.

I ended up taking a detour into the fence on the left that had an open gate. I ran down the dark dirt road for survival. After a while, I finally noticed I was by myself when I didn't hear footsteps behind me. I looked up ahead and noticed a pretty large tree. I went to it to catch my breath and used this as a chance to look back for my friends. I looked back and saw all three of my friends limping, slowly approaching me. I started to panic, so I ran toward them to close the distance. I remembered hearing three gunshots, and all three of my friends were staggering. I finally got to them and instantly asked them if they were hit. I began to check them for wounds and blood.

I noticed everyone seemed OK but was drenched in sweat. I checked myself and my friends to make sure no one got hit, especially because when adrenaline hits, you really don't realize pain until the body slows down. After I asked if they were all right, one of them finally responded to me and said, "Nah, man, we didn't get shot, but we tired as hell." Turns out these fools were just winded, exhausted, and breathing heavily because of the running. Still aware of my surroundings, I looked back toward the entrance of the gate we ran into and didn't see the four guys anymore.

Reunited now, we asked the combined question, "What happened?" to one another.

"Well, I don't know. I heard three gunshots and took off." Everyone was OK. Then the situation set in on us. Damn, we just got shot at, and nothing hit us. Nervous, wondering if they were still attempting to follow us in the distance, we continued to walk to the party. Now time-out, with all that shit that just happened not even a minute earlier, we were still on the way to the party. Ironically, we noticed that we got to the party faster. The building was in plain sight with the music blasting. Once we realized that we were close, we simultaneously looked down at our shoes and then our outfits—shoe tips all creased, mud and dirt on the sides, armpits sweating and all. We looked back up at each other without saying a word, smiled, and said, "Man, we in here. Fuck that."

Less was said, as all were in nonverbal agreement that we were going to the party to have a good time regardless of what had just taken place. We finally got to the entrance and paid our twenty-dollar entry fee. The dude who took our money at the door looked at us like we were fucking lost. But "Man, we in here. Fuck that." And what do you know? We walked in just in time for the twerking music.

* * *

A part of being in college was going to parties—not just local parties in the city but other college parties in different states. So that meant road trips. I drove a pretty big SUV that my friends commonly referred to as "the bus." It had seven seats, a lot of leg space, and was reliable for the most part. I loved that truck. Having a car in college is definitely a blessing and a burden. People always want a ride somewhere. After a while, you find yourself becoming a taxi driver for your friends because they always want to go somewhere. Just because *I* had a car, that meant *we* had a car in their heads. But the part that really gets me is that they would never offer to help on gas. I could spend an entire chapter talking about how raggedy friends are, but let me tell this story first.

It was a Saturday night with my boys. And you know how we do. We decided earlier that morning that we were going to make a road trip to South Carolina for a party. It was about an hour-and-a-half drive so I knew off rip this would be a long night. Without even conversing about how we would get there, these dudes already assumed that we were taking my truck. How does that work? One of my friends even stood up to say, "Nigga, we taking the bus. What you mean?"

You could see the confusion on my face from a mile away. "All right, man, fine, damn," was my response to the group. I didn't mind driving at all honestly because I didn't trust too many people with my life behind the wheel. So I got it that night, but I knew driving to a party in another state brought obligation. Not only would I be the designated driver, which meant being sober throughout the night, but I was also the unspoken babysitter for the night, making sure that the group who rode with me wasn't sloppy drunk, not picking fights with people or trying to holla at other folks' girls. That was now my obligation. All right, whatever, but I told them and myself that I was going to have fun that night. I can vividly remember saying to them, "Man, I'm not babysitting nobody tonight. I'm getting on some girls tonight. Fuck what you heard."

The look they gave me was the same look you would give a kid who asks the teacher if they're collecting the homework from last night. They looked at me and said, "Mannn, shut yo sweet ass up…" and a lot more things, but that's not important right now.

If you can recall, earlier in chapter 5, I talked about the phases of a party. Well, there was nothing different about this night. Phases I and II were in full effect. We went to the liquor store to get our liq [Inject: liq is short for liquor] for the night. Everybody was on hard liquor as normal before a party, but I was on something sweet and light, also per usual. But you can't drink on an empty stomach, so we drove down the street to get some four-for-fours.

After we got our food, we hit the road to South Carolina for the party. My truck had seven seats to include the driver's seat, so guess how many people were in the car that night. That's right! You guessed it. It was a full car. I had six of my homeboys riding with me to the party. The car was filled with food, liquor, music, and dope energy.

On the way to the party, I had the music turned hard as fuck. We were eating burgers and passing around shots to each other, having a great time. Now, your eyebrows probably just arched. I was the designated driver. I didn't take any shots while I was driving. Don't worry; my irresponsible part comes in a little later.

As I followed my GPS, I got off the highway and progressed down this back road. I was a little skeptical going this way because I had never taken a back road at night to get to South Carolina, and there were no streetlights along the road. Plus, the part of South Carolina we were heading to was country, so along the way, I noticed a shit ton of deer on both sides of the road as we drove through. Now my phone was going in and out of service, so my GPS did a lot of reconnecting.

While I was driving and contemplating all of the above, my buddies were steadily eating and rapping Future songs on the aux cord, not paying attention to shit I was seeing. Again, that was the reason I was driving because I only trusted myself with my life behind the wheel of a car.

After about thirty minutes of looking at deer on the side of the road, driving on this unlit road with my friends in the back talking shit about nothing, I looked ahead and could see the location of the party. I turned the music down in the car and could hear the music from the party up the street. The parking lot was crowded with cars, so I could tell this was gonna be piped. I struggled to find parking with all these damn cars but eventually found a spot toward the back of the lot.

As I pulled up to the parking spot, girls were getting out of their cars and heading toward the party. Man, you talk about bad. Of course, my ignorant friends were hanging out the windows trying to make plays before we even stepped foot out of the car.

Finally, we got to the parking spot, and it was time to have a great night. We got inside the party, and I literally couldn't see anything—not because it was that dark inside but because there was so much ass in this dwelling. Yes, dwelling, 'cause, my lord. I was thinking to myself that I should transfer to this college. I didn't know South Carolina was packing like that; it was almost unbelievable. But like I mentioned earlier, I was going to have fun tonight. "Fuck what you heard." I started dancing, getting danced on, taking a few shots here and there, and getting a few phone numbers while I was at it. This one girl was so fine I remember telling her, "Aye, you might want to be with me… My future lit as fuck." This was after a few shots so I guess that was liquid courage giving me the strength to say some shit like that. But hey, how does the saying go? "A drunk man tells no tales." So I wasn't lying when I said it. I was lit and having a great time talking my talk.

As the party started to come to an end, people were of course promoting different after-parties to go to. Just like we talked about earlier in chapter 5, phase IV of the night, kids just don't know how to go home. There had to be a party after the party. At this point in the night, it was about 2:30 a.m., and we still had a good hour-and-a-half drive back to Savannah. So we collectively opted not to go to the after-parties and head back. That was probably the only smart decision we made all night.

We got to my car, and all of us were torn up, including me, but I was focused enough to at minimum get us back home. Even after taking shots at the party, my sober instinct kicked in to get us home safe. I drove out of the parking lot, and the first turn I made brought me down the same exact unlit road before hitting the highway. I put my high beams on and turned the music down, but left it loud enough to keep me up. I had both hands on the steering wheel as I drove down the dark road. Again, just like the drive up there, I noticed families of deer along the side. It was still a little alarming to me, but I stayed focused on the road. I looked in my rearview mirror and saw that all these negroes in the back were knocked out asleep, to include my friend in the passenger seat. He was supposed to be my assistant driver, my codriver, helping me stay awake, but this man was out cold. Aight, bet no worries, I got this.

I was doing about forty-five miles per hour down this road, and the maximum speed was fifty, so I wasn't violating the law at all. I felt something within, something telling me to slow down a little. I couldn't. I was determined to make it back as fast as possible because I felt myself nodding off here and there while behind the wheel.

This was just all bad, but I had about another ten minutes on this back road before turning onto the highway. The road was too dark. It was late, and as much as I was fighting my eyelids to stay open, I found myself nodding off more and more. After a couple of nods, I gave myself a pep talk to stay awake. I was almost at the highway, where I could hopefully concentrate better. Plus, I didn't want to get stuck on this back road with no lighting or cell phone service. I looked up and saw what looked like a deer in the middle of the road. *Oh shit! It is a deer!* I didn't have much time to respond.

By the time I noticed the deer, it was about thirty feet in front of the car. I was going forty-five miles per hour. In the spilt second I had to respond, I did what you are never supposed to do to avoid a deer. I violently turned my steering wheel in the direction the damn deer was going. Then it was like the deer recognized that I was turning because it decided to react too. The deer jetted off, trying not to get hit, and somehow launched its body in the same direction I turned my car. Bam! I hit the deer. Still with my foot on the gas, I was crossing the next lane going forty miles per hour. When I finally realized what was going on, I struggled to slow the car down. I was slowing down, but it obviously wasn't quick enough because I drove off the road onto the other side of traffic into the dirt.

Somehow, by the grace of God, I was able to get control of the car to bring it back toward the road and avoid hitting a tree while on the dirt side of the road. I finally made it back on the road to a point where I could completely stop the car. In disbelief at what had just happened, I looked back in my rearview mirror to see if the deer was still in sight. There it was, lying in the middle of the road. I really looked back in the rearview mirror to make sure there wasn't a support group of deer coming to help the one I had just murdered before getting out of my car. The coast was clear.

I stepped out of my car and immediately walked over to see the front of my hood. When I made it to the front, my heart skipped a beat. The sound of the impact didn't reflect the damage actually done because the front of my car was smashed in with blood scattered on the hood. It looked like someone had taken a bulldozer and swung it into the front of my car. The entire front side of my car was fucked. I walked a little toward the deer I hit and noticed it was lying there not moving. With no cell phone service to call anyone and, let's be real, a group of seven black college kids leaving a party and smelling like alcohol wasn't the best narrative. So I told everyone to get back into the car, and I drove off. I was wide the fuck awake now. I pulled off and stayed on the road about another five minutes and then saw the highway.

I turned on the highway, and forty-five minutes later, we were back in Savannah and back on camp around 4:30 a.m. After dropping everyone off, I went to park my car. I was just happy that we were able to make it back in one piece. I was going to deal with the damages done that night later in the morning. I got to my room and immediately laid down fully clothed.

A little later in the morning, around 11:00 a.m., after getting some sleep, I walked out to the car to see how bad my car really was. A part of me just thought that everything that had happened with the party and the deer was just a dream, a terrible dream, and I would walk out to my car to see everything intact just how I had last seen it. No, I wasn't dreaming. My car was bad. The external damage was really bad so I imagined that I had screwed up something major on the inside. I noticed that the latch of the hood was broken, so essentially, the hood had been open the entire drive back last night. Damn, I drove back last night with my hood unsecured. It could have easily flown open while I was driving at any point last night and caused a worse situation.

I opened the hood to look inside, and there was a lot wrong. A bunch of leaves and sticks were in the hood in random areas. I guess that happened when I veered off to the side of the road. I looked to see the fan that cooled the engine was snapped in half, and I had an oil leak that had emptied itself overnight. I wasn't too savvy with cars, but against my better judgment, with everything wrong, I decided to start the car. As soon as she started up, smoke came from the engine. So before I could blow myself up, I took the keys out of the ignition and walked away.

I was thinking to myself, *What the fuck did I just do? I just messed up my means of transportation and for what? A good time? Nah, it's not worth it.* I had a totaled car with no way or money to get it towed and fixed. Where were my buddies who rode with me to help with this? Understand this: if you get yourself into a situation, no matter how many of your friends are there with you, you better be ready to fend for yourself and get yourself out of that situation by yourself. A couple of days later, I started the car again, and she started, with no smoke.

Before it could start smoking or worse, I decided to drive to a mechanic shop about ten minutes away. I got there, and I had the mechanics assess the damage done and the cost to get it fixed. I was worried more about the internal damages, like fixing the fan to cool the engine, so I wouldn't explode while driving, more than I was focused on the body of the car.

To fix the damages done to the inside of the car was $1,500 dollars. Of course, I didn't have that kind of money just sitting around, and I refused to place this burden on my mom. A few options ran through my head, but none would get me far. I finally decided to get a credit card, my very first one. Ironically, since this was my first credit card with no past history or report, the credit card company started me off with the minimum amount—$1,500. I maxed out that card fixing the car with no immediate way to pay it off. I guessed I'd figure that part out later.

CHAPTER 6

IT GETS BETTER

Graduating from college was easily one of the best days of my life. I had accomplished a lot of things. I made new friends who I still keep in touch with today, made great memories, and had tremendous experiences. Ironically, this was also one of the worst times I can remember. I was proud of myself for getting my degree, which was the ultimate goal, but I felt so ashamed and embarrassed this day too. I had worked my ass off to finish my two-for-one deal that I had ran so hard for over the course of four years. And I threw it all away making dumb decisions.

May 7, 2016, 9:30 a.m., Tiger Stadium—I'll never forget it. This was the day I walked across that graduation stage to receive my bachelor of science degree in criminal justice, something I had put in late hours for and was proud that I had accomplished. But this day, I wasn't receiving my commission in the United States Navy. I made some dumb decisions that took it from me—exactly one week before graduation day. I couldn't be mad or upset with anyone but myself, and that was when I understood my growth as a man. I took responsibility for the fuck-ups in *my* life, because it was my life. If I make a good decision, that's on me, and if I make a poor decision, then that's on me as well. I owned my life, so that meant owning my decisions, good or bad. And the hard part meant not blaming other people for the situations I got myself into.

During the graduation ceremony, it was customary to present the newest commissioned officers in the Navy and Marine Corps to the enormous crowd in attendance. As I was sitting in the crowd with my class and I watched my peers walk onto the stage as their names were called, in their summer whites, looking amazing.

I couldn't have been any prouder of them for making it to the goal we all set out to achieve when we were freshmen. These were my same comrades I trained with at 4:00 a.m. most mornings, getting yelled at by our Marine Corps instructor. They were the people I studied with before tests late nights, ate with, and bonded with for four years to achieve what we came to do. I looked down at the program, and it had all of their names listed, to include mine. I was supposed to be on that stage too.

My classmates on my row and behind me noticed my name on the program and shrugged their shoulders at me to ask, "What happened? Why aren't you up there?"

Embarrassed, I whispered over while making hand gestures, "Mine got pushed back. I gotta finish up a class."

They would nod off to my response and say OK, but I knew in my heart that this chapter of my life was over before it had even started. Damn, I screwed up.

Let me back-track to the week prior to graduation day. I remember this like it was yesterday because of the hurt and pain that I felt. Really this sticks with me because of how it affected my mom, who gave a lot to make sure I had what needed to thrive. April 30, 2016, the Saturday before the big day, I was at a frat party my bruhs hosted on camp. This was the last party of the semester and my last party as an undergrad, so I was there in full effect. But in the same breath, I was playing my actions at the party safe because I did not want to risk getting in trouble for anything, especially being the week before graduation and commission. So, I was at the front table taking tickets and collecting money outside the doors of the party for most of the night. College kids were trickling in from other fraternities, sororities, and organizations from other schools. Music was blasting, booties were shaking, shit was lit. I was at the front table so I could see everyone who was coming into the party. I noticed my ex-girlfriend walk up with another girl to go into the party. Now this wasn't an ordinary breakup, but to say the least, she and I had a restraining order on campus to stay six feet apart. She pulled up to this party already knowing that, but whatever, there was less than a week of undergrad left. I wasn't trippin'. Enjoy the party.

Without exchanging words, I took her money for the entrance fee into the party and left it at that. Three hours went by, and it was nearing the end of the party. Plus, it was on camp so it ended around 1:30 a.m. or so. People started to break out, heading towards their cars to leave. The parking lot started to clear out. As that was happening, I was joking around with my frat brothers, cleaning up and talking about how the party was a success. Another thirty minutes passed by, and the parking lot had cleared with the exception of our cars parked out front. One of my friends pointed to a car parked in the distance, still sitting there. I looked only to realize that the car still parked there was my ex's car. *What the fuck?* was going through my head. I was confused as shit as to why she was there, especially sitting off in the cut how she was.

I decided to leave the party with my homeboy Dez, who also came to the party. We got in his car and drove off. I told him to drop me off at my dorm room, which was on campus. As we were headed there, I was texting a young lady I was heavily involved with sexually and emotionally to meet me in front of my room. Dez and I pulled up outside of my dorm room, and there was Porsha in front of us, sitting in her car waiting for me to get her. Before I opened my door to step out of Dez's ride, I noticed my ex's car hostilely pull up directly behind us. I was really confused and nervous as hell at this point, so I didn't get out of the car. Instead, I told Dez to drive off. I texted Porsha and told her Alicia had pulled up behind me from nowhere. I was going to go off camp for a minute to stop a situation before it became a situation.

We made a left turn at the first stop light and were off campus on a long two-way road, and still, Alicia was behind us, tailing us at that point. I could feel the aggression, and tension had escalated very quickly so Dez sped up to see what this really was. Essentially so we could determine if this really turned into a situation— And yep, this was now a situation. Once we noticed that it, this had escalated to an all-out car chase. Dez hit the gas. He drove a Camaro so we sped up fast.

We turned into this unlit Section Eight housing complex to calm the situation down. Thinking that we had lost her when we sped up, here she came speeding into the complex, blocking us in from leaving. The complex we had pulled into just happened to be a cul-de-sac, a dead end, so we were blocked in. Alicia got out of her car, heated, and angrily stormed to the passenger side where I was sitting. She started screaming and banging on the window as hard as fuck—so hard that Dez and I thought she was going to smash his window.

This was obviously a bad situation now because the neighborhood lights were coming on, and people were waking up from their sleep to see what was going on. Alicia was yelling outside through the window at me, "Come out the car, bitch!"

I was yelling back at her from inside the car, "Hell nah, dummy! What the fuck is wrong with you, bro?" I decided to take my phone out and record this whole ordeal. Why'd I do that? She got even more pissed. During this whole thing, I couldn't think about why this was happening or even what I did to be put in this current position. I was too busy focusing on how to get the fuck out of it.

After fifteen minutes of Alicia and I banging on the window, yelling, cussing, and screaming at each other back and forth, Dez and I saw a little wiggle room between Alicia's car and the curb that we could squeeze through, and we did just that. We squeezed through, almost running her foot over in the process. Then we sped up and headed back to camp. We turned into campus and waited in the line to show our IDs to the security guard to get back on. Once we got to the security guard, I looked back and saw that she was a few cars back. Now I was really saying to myself, "What the fuck is happening right now?"

I said to the security guard, "There is a girl a few cars back who doesn't live on campus. Don't let her on."

That was the rule anyway. Off-campus students weren't supposed to be on after a certain hour. At this point, I was trying my best to diffuse the situation but obviously nothing I did helped. I was looking back through the mirror as I said this and noticed she was now out of her car, approaching us. The security guard, I could tell, was overwhelmed at the situation with all these college kids and their drama, so he told us to pull over to the side.

A couple of minutes later, the campus police pulled up and tried to figure out what exactly was happening. I guess we were in the same boat because I was trying to figure out the same.

Confused still, I didn't know what to say except "Man, I'm just trying to go home."

I didn't have to say much because Alicia was in the background still yelling. I listened to her words to see if I could figure out exactly why was she was so upset. But there was no root cause that I heard; it was just pure anger. The police had had enough at this point and directed her to leave campus. I had a good relationship with them, so they told Dez to drop me off at my room and leave because he couldn't stay on camp either. All of this, from the time the party ended to when I finally made it to my room, was forty-five minutes. So many thoughts, so much confusion on my part, I still didn't understand what had happened and why. We had a restraining order on campus, so there wasn't anything to talk about. Man, I don't know.

Monday rolled around. It was May 2, 2016, the week of graduation and commissioning. My mom was coming Thursday to be present for Friday's commissioning ceremony and Saturday's commencement. A few other people my mom was close to who wanted to come and support us were coming too. Four years of hard work and bullshit was finally ending. I was ready to move forward in my life.

Later in the morning on that Monday, Porsha came to my room. I thought it was to kick it, but it was to tell me that she went to my NROTC chain of command and told them about the chase and everything that happened last Saturday. One thing I did not mention was that she was there during the chase, being stuck in the dead end all the way up to getting back on campus that night. A part of the yelling and screaming in the housing complex was because Porsha was there. Awwwwww, OK, we getting somewhere now, but I'll come back to that point. Porsha told me that she told my chain of command everything that happened. She pointed out that she did it to exploit my ex's actions and involvement in outlandish behavior. Oh yeah, Alicia was in NROTC program as well.

Although I understood her intentions and that she tried to isolate me as much as possible from her story to my chain of command, I knew nothing good was going to come out of her doing that.

Damn, bro. "Why the hell did you do that?" was my reaction. I was gonna let it ride and not say shit. "You gotta understand we've had a history of issues, so to have another one a week before graduation come to their attention isn't smart at all" was what I told Porsha. Then again, no police report or anything in black and white was signed, so there was no evidence that anything happened. Her telling my chain of command was out of complete frustration on her part and was not aimed to make the unthinkable happen. I understood and believed that.

The week of graduation/commissioning, the ROTC instructors gave the seniors that week off, free of classes and physical training to focus on getting everything ready for the ceremonies. Tuesday morning, I got a call from one of my instructors to come see him as quick as humanly possible. I was in my room when he called, so I headed over to see what was up. I got to his office, and he asked me to close the door behind me. This could only be about one thing, and my heart began to pound harder. He didn't ask me any questions about anything that had taken place the previous weekend. He said to me, "Whatever happened on Saturday, just know that we are launching an investigation."

In my mind, I was assuming that wouldn't take long obviously because I did commission in three days. Shortly after he told me about the investigation, he said, "Because we have to do this investigation due to the decisions you decided to make a week before commencement, you will not commission Friday."

And my heart dropped. *Not like this man, I can't lose what I worked for like this.* Once he dismissed me from his office, I went straight to my room. I sat on the bed to digest the news. With hotel rooms booked and arrangements made for my family to come into town, I had no idea how I was going to tell my mom I screwed up, bad. I didn't have the courage or strength to tell her that day, so I waited. A lot of it was because I still didn't believe it myself.

The next day, I attended my last chapter meeting as an undergrad to discuss end-of-the-year business and to debrief the party. Halfway through the meeting, my phone started ringing, so I stepped out to answer it. It just so happened to be my mom calling. I didn't answer before it went to voice mail, so I called her back just as I stepped out of the room. She answered in very high spirits. She was upbeat and sounded very excited for the weekend. My mom normally always told me how proud of me she was, and this phone call was no different. She told me how proud she was that I had turned out to be something positive in life, a role model, that I had a good career lined up now, and topped it off by saying, "I love you."

I was overwhelmed with emotions because I knew I had to tell her what was going on, but I still didn't have the audacity or jaw strength to fix my mouth to deliver the news. But it had to be done. "Ma, there is something I need to tell you."

"What it is it, Son?" was her response.

I took a deep breath and let it all out. As a son, one thing that I absolutely can't deal with is when my mom cries, and to be the source of her tears destroyed me. I could hear her voice trembling, trying to speak words, and she eventually made the emotions plain. Her tears hurt me through the phone. That was the worst fifteen seconds of my life, telling my mom disappointing news like that. It hurt me even more because I knew how much this lady sacrificed for me to even be alive let alone to have these unexpected opportunities in life, which I essentially just threw away. All I wanted to do was make her proud, but I had screwed that up by trying to be the man on campus.

Self-reflection hit me. All I could say to my mom was "I am sorry, Mama. I am so sorry. I messed up." I repeated that a couple of times.

Nonetheless, I was still graduating with my degree Saturday, and that was still something to be excited about. I had accomplished a goal that hadn't been achieved in my family before. I was the first. Our emotions had calmed down after ten minutes of tension, and even in the midst of it, my mom showed me something that is hard to get from people. She told me that everything was going to work out, to keep my head high, and that she would be there Thursday as planned to be with me. She showed me unconditional love that night. Despite the stupid decisions I had made over the course of a week and what it cost me, she still had my back. But I had to fix this somehow. In the end, this was my life that I had to figure out, but it was nice to have someone in my corner who would help guide and support me to make the right decisions but also have my back when I chose wrong. This was definitely a low time in my life. I had to make sense of my decisions and, most important, figure out the lesson in all of this.

The Monday after graduation day, my future as a naval officer was undetermined. At this point, my fate was out of my hands. All I could do was hope and pray that everything would work out. The investigation began, and as far as I knew, it consisted of getting witness statements, video surveillance, and even the video I recorded in the car the night of the car chase, everything—all of this to determine if I would commission or not. I could tell by the intensity and extensiveness of the investigation that this was not looking good for me.

I am not one to waste time with my life so to be better prepared if this turned out negatively, I started applying for jobs in the civilian sector. I think one job I applied for was to be a correctional officer at a local jail in Savannah. Thank God I didn't get a callback for that job because I would have been eaten alive in there. Along with applying for jobs, I applied to different colleges to pursue a master's, preparing for a change in plans. A month went by—no responses on jobs, nor did I know my future in the navy. I ended up staying in Savannah to stay local in case I needed to go to the ROTC unit at any moment. I wasn't working, had no money, and was way too embarrassed to ask my mom for money to support me in the meantime. Really, I felt undeserving. I had gotten myself into this mess, and I needed to figure out how to get myself out. I moved into the one-story, four-bedroom house my frat brothers were living in. It was close to the unit, and they had an extra bedroom, so it worked out all right.

Day to day, my scheduled consisted of absolutely nothing. I slept, played basketball to stay sane, ate when I could, but mostly did a lot of waiting around. Every day, I was waiting on a miracle to happen someway somehow. I went to the ROTC building when necessary or to sign paperwork. But I stayed close and didn't work at all because if I got a call during the day to come in, I wanted to be readily available. I guess you can say I put this imaginary job as my top responsibility.

I didn't have steady money to eat for a solid two months, so I started to pawn my belongings for cash. There was a pawn shop up the street, so I started with my old television. I got about twenty bucks for that. The twenty dollars lasted me about a week, but I had to really be frugal, considering I had to put in gas my car and eat. I ate very sparingly, dollar menus and cheap gas station foods. There were times I ate once a day whether it was a dollar burger or chips I'd snack on throughout the day, or I just didn't eat that day at all. It was a shitty situation, but I could not feel bad for myself at all. This was what I deserved. And I damn sure wasn't going to move back home. I had to figure this shit out and begin to establish my own.

The next week, I pawned my Xbox 360 and video games to go with it, not much at all, roughly forty-five dollars for everything, but I had to do what I had to, on my own to eat.

After another few weeks of pawning stuff for cash, June 21, 2016, at 7:00 p.m., I got a call from my instructor to come to the unit the next day dressed in khakis. I sensed this was it. This was the decision that I was being called in to hear. Whether good or bad, it was time to move forward. After a month and a half of depression and uncertainty about my future, I was ready to hear the verdict. The next day, Wednesday morning, I walked into the unit head held high in khakis, standing by for the commanding officer. Ten minutes elapsed, and he called me into his office. As I walked in, my attention went to his desk for some reason, and I noticed paperwork sticking out of a manila folder. That was immediately a bad sign. Those were my release papers inside. I didn't freak out. I didn't panic. I sat down in a chair directly in front of him, looked down at the folder, looked up at him, and said, "Good morning, sir."

He cut straight to the chase and let me have it. He was extremely disappointed in my behavior, and so was I. He then told me to open the manila folder sitting in front of me, and there was my commissioning paperwork. Filled with joy and all kinds of emotions, I damn near fainted in the chair. All that ran through my mind was this: *All of the trouble I caused myself, the stress I put on my family, and the shame I brought to everyone and my CO still believes in me? He still believes I can come back from this and make a positive impact on the world? I won't let you down. I am done with letting people down.*

Immediately after, I called my mom and told her, and you can imagine her response and how that conversation went. It was a hard message, but one I read loud and clear, one that needed to happen for my personal growth and development as a man.

*   *   *

See, the thing about life is that you never know how big the bumps in the road are until you see the damage to your car. A lot of things that happen in our lives force us to slow down to take a hard look at ourselves and where we are going. I believe this lesson was twofold: I had gotten myself into some situations that I never saw coming, all because I was trying to be something I wasn't. Those two ladies, Porsha and Alicia, aren't to blame for anything. I am. The huge lesson I took from that experience is say what you mean but, more important, show what you say. Sounds easy enough to do, as if it's second nature, and that's great if you're thinking that way. But there comes a day when you have to deal with yourself.

Sending mixed signals, saying one thing but doing another is the quickest way to find yourself in a bad situation. With everything in my situation, it happened so fast that I never got the opportunity to express to those two ladies this: I am sorry. Looking back, I see clearly the mistakes I made that caused the entire thing to blow up the way it did. I take full responsibility for the part I played to escalate these situations to what they were. I am so sorry. I can't really right my wrongs at this point, but the least I can do is acknowledge those screw-ups. It simply boils down to this: "When I was a *child*, I used to speak like a *child*, think like a *child*, reason like a *child*; when I became a man, I did away with childish things" (1 Corinthians 13:11).

*   *   *

One thing about being financially able for me was oriented toward helping people who needed it—not really being financially stable because that shouldn't be the only time you can lend a helping hand but more so being warm in having a genuine heart to be able to give and help others. It didn't matter who you were or where I was. I talked to strangers off the street and homeless people who would not get a second look from others walking by. That could easily be me on the side of the street or any one of us. It doesn't make them any less human than I am.

My mom used to always ask me when I was growing up why I would be the last person coming on the bus or even the last person to eat at the lunch table. Without realizing it then, I wanted to make sure others got on the bus and seated where they wanted first. I wanted to make sure others got what they wanted to eat at lunch before they ran out of food. I didn't really care too much if I got what was left. Sounds crazy, I know. Why in the world would I even think that way? I could ask you the same question reversed. Why is it that you don't think that way? Why don't we put others' well-being before our own? A lot of the way we think is selfish, and it's the *I-got-to-get-mine* approach. I've learned and accepted that those early stages of my youth putting others before myself weren't a phase. It was a glimpse into the man I would become in this world.

One sunny Saturday San Diego afternoon—that's a mouthful, I know; stay with me for this story—I slept in after a long week at work. I woke up hungry as ever and craved some IHOP. I had one up the street from my apartment, so I called my order in to-go and left my place to pick it up about fifteen minutes later. I got to IHOP, and there the food was, ready for me to pick up and take. After leaving there with my food, I couldn't wait to get back home to eat and go right back to sleep. Because there was limited parking where I stayed, I parked my car down the street from my spot and walked the rest of the way. And what happened on my two-minute walk home changed my way of thinking.

I saw a homeless man walking on the same side of the street toward me. I could tell he wasn't walking directly toward me but just strolling through minding his business. As he got closer, within speaking distance, he quickly noticed the IHOP bag I was carrying. He opened his mouth and asked, "Is that for me?" I got the vibe he asked it jokingly but was somewhat serious too, or else he wouldn't have asked that from a stranger.

Still walking toward my place, I took a glance at him and responded, "Nah, man, this is for me; I'm hungry," as I continued to walk. He grinned slightly and walked off, and I continued about my day. I took another couple of steps and stopped right where I stood. I looked back in the direction of the man and saw him continue to walk. After thinking to myself, I realized how quickly I had fallen off my path. Because I was so focused on myself and getting back home to eat, I couldn't even look someone in the eyes and help him along the way. I turned around and yelled, "Excuse me, sir! Excuse me!"

He turned to look at me, and I began to close the distance between us. Once I got closer, I said, "Hey, this actually is for you." I handed the bag of food to him and started to describe everything that was in it.

With a tremble in his voice, he said, "Really? This is for me?"

I said, "Yes, sir, you enjoy. Be safe, and God bless."

Now whether he was homeless or really wasn't, whether he was hungry or wasn't, whether this was staged to get free stuff from people wasn't my concern. I zoomed out and looked at the bigger picture. This was definitely a small act of kindness and could've been easily regarded as "just food." In retrospect, that is exactly what it was, just giving him some food. But check this: it wasn't about the bag of IHOP or the money spent to get the food. It was about giving to someone else I knew I could help. For me, I could easily just eat something else, and that's exactly what I did. I went into my apartment and warmed up some noodles. However, for that gentleman, that might have been the first hot meal he'd had in a while or even his last meal for the foreseeable future. Who knows? But that's not for the giver to figure out.

My job was to help how and where I could so that was exactly what I did. I knew I couldn't live with myself not doing my part and giving what essentially was given to me. And I'm not talking about the food, but the act of showing a kind, genuine heart. That day, I reminded myself that it is OK to give a shit about another person, despite what you are going through.

Afterward, I had to call someone I trusted, so I called my mom and told her what had just happened. I wasn't looking for praise or a pat on the back, knowing I did something positive. My reason for calling her was for reassurance. "Mom, tell me it's not crazy to care about another human being, about a complete stranger."

At this point, as I shared what had happened, I started to get choked up while on the phone because everything was hitting me at once. I just began to thank God for putting me in this position in life and in that position to give earlier that day. It was a great deed, but in the grand scheme of things, the well-being of the person to the left and right should be just as important as our own. It's a hard thing to consider and an even tougher idea to perform. But consider this: be that hand to reach out and help someone in their situation because you never really know what someone is contemplating. The same genuineness you show people just might trickle down. They just might have the heart and means to help someone else. The saying is true: *In order to change the world, we must change ourselves first.*

CHAPTER 7

HOW WILL YOUR STORY BEGIN?

Well, this is an awkward way to title a chapter, I know. In some respects, you have no control over how your life will shape out. Some things just do or don't happen to you. But what you do control is your narrative. You control your pitch. You control the aspects of your life that you want to share with the world. Where you choose to start that story, well, that depends on you. As for myself, the journey to becoming me wasn't easy. There were good times, there were trying times, and there were flat-out bad times. But it all depends on how you choose to navigate through those situations.

Don't wait to tell your story. It doesn't need to be polished or edited. It really doesn't even need to be perfect. And that's honestly what makes it perfect. What it does need to be is true and authentic to you. Not every story has to be about drugs or gangs for it to reach people's minds. Telling a story is about changing lives. How you do that is by sharing any and all of your experiences, and, more important, by highlighting the experiences—the goods, bads, and uglies—and expressing how they helped mold you into the person you are or how they are molding you into the person you are destined to become.

You might not know or realize it, but someone needs to hear that they aren't alone in what they are going through. Never be ashamed of what made you, *you*. Interestingly enough, you know what the future and the past have in common? You're currently writing both. And while you're writing them, be sure you include the part in there to make certain they remember you were here.

Throughout this memoir and throughout my life, I shared different experiences that helped shape my mind and subsequently my goals in life. I understood how the things I was going through could impact my future, but only if I let them. You see, just because life hits you one way does not mean you have to allow it to continue. You are that chosen one who is destined to break the cycle of depression, hatred, and every filthy thing this dreadful world has to offer. The way you do that comes from telling your story.

Even in writing this book, Microsoft Word is giving me suggestions on how I should structure my sentences, highlighting misspellings, pointing out sentence fragments, and telling me to delete words. That's the program's job, but just like people, they'll tell you what you need to do and how you should do things. They will tell you how to write, what to do, how to do. But never forget you are the writer of your story, so thank you for telling me how I should be, but I decide to be what I choose. I wrote this how I wanted, regardless of what anyone had to say. Tell the world where the fuck you from. Tell the world what the fuck you've been through. But essentially, tell the world how you overcame your struggles. You can probably sense the passion in those sentences, but I'm serious. Your story is important because it may be the one thing a young child or even someone in their forties needs to hear to keep them in the fight. What will you *say* to get their attention? Better question, what will you *do* to keep it? Experience doesn't have a particular age attached to it. Whether you learn something early in life or later in life, the lesson is on time for you and your growth.

I've had to grow up in a single-parent home with no love from a man, dealing with death, denial, homelessness, birth deformities, and many breakdowns, but here is what I can say. I didn't let the beginning determine my end. In the same breath, a story isn't always about the bad times because there are lessons in the good times too. I often prayed for the rain to stop in my life, forgetting that I would still have to deal with the mud. In other words, it is not going to be easy, and anything worth having has to be worth the work. It has to be worth a little bit of blood, some sweat, and a lot of tears. Tears are signs of passion when you work your ass off to get where you want to in life. You should feel tears of passion, a sense of pride, and the feeling of accomplishment I feel right now just thinking about this journey. I need you to follow your dreams and allow your individuality to shine on the world. Your existence and your purpose were determined before you ever realized it. Understand this, especially to the young African American generation reading this: you can be a doctor, surgeon, lawyer, author, dentist, and anything under the sun. Find what that thing is for you, and be your absolute best. Tomorrow is not promised. Work hard now so you can take it easy later. Revisit this chapter when you need that reminder.

A lot of the stories I've shared through and through have been personal to me. Some were sad stories, and some were happy stories. No matter if I thought the story was too minute to include in this book, I owe it to myself and you reading this not to hold back. I think that is the scariest part of it all, being scared. The "what-if's," per se. What if people don't feel me? Or what if writing this book is a dumb idea? Funny thing, that is exactly what I thought before starting this memoir. Before putting my pen to paper, I constantly let myself talk my own self out of following my passion to write. Most of the time, our biggest restraint is our own thoughts. I talked down on this idea to write this and discouraged myself, believing that no one needed to hear this from me, believing that this had already been done by numerous people, so what's the point? Although that may be true, it hasn't been done by *you*. And believe it or not, that's what people are waiting for, to hear from you.

When those negative thoughts came in, I told that part of myself to shut the fuck up, and the other part of me went to work. I was in a constant battle with myself, but I knew I couldn't give up; I couldn't give in. When you hear that portion of your mind telling you that you can't do something or it's not worth the try, realize that this is your first and last shot at life. Chase your dreams. The best thing you can do is believe you can, and then do the damn thing. But all in all, the culmination of the stories throughout this book helped to tell my story of what made Torrey, Torrey. In the end, you got somewhat of a taste of my approach on life. My philosophy is this: life is 10 percent of what happens to you and 90 percent of how you respond to what happens to you.

This life we live is a journey, an adventure with mysteries that we solve every day. It isn't meant to be easy, nor does it come with any written scripts. Through the great and awful times come lessons that we can learn from. The lessons we learn are only as good as the action behind them and the effort not to repeat the same mistakes. People only tell you what you can't do because they can't do it.

*   *   *

My daughter, Aubrey Yvette Butler, was born! On July 14, 2020, she came out seven pounds fifteen ounces and 20.5 inches long with all ten fingers and ten toes. She is so beautiful, and

I absolutely fell in love that day. My pride and joy gave me a new outlook on life coming into mine. I was overwhelmed and extremely emotional watching my daughter in that delivery room. Cutting the umbilical cord and holding her for the first time melted my heart down to the ground. I never knew I could feel this type of love for another human being until I laid eyes on Aubrey. This easily would've been the best day of my life, being there for the birth of my firstborn baby girl. It's a shame I wasn't there. I missed my baby girl's introduction into the world. I missed my opportunity to be emotional watching my daughter in the delivery room. I missed my chance to cut the umbilical cord and hold her for the first time so my heart could melt to the ground. I watched my daughter come into the world from a computer screen, through pictures sent to my email address.

Twenty-six years old and I swore to myself that things would different with me as a father. I swore I'd never turn out like my dad. So much for wanting different in my own life, because I am off to a great start! I guess the apple doesn't fall far from the tree. My father wasn't there for my birth, and I wasn't there for my own child's so that makes me no different in my eyes. I understand I'm probably being hard on myself. Although my situation was different from my father's, it still does not take away the fact that Daddy wasn't there. Where was I when you were born Aubrey? Deployed, baby girl, in the middle of the Eastern Pacific Ocean / Caribbean Sea, in my rack holding a pink teddy bear that has a recording of your heartbeat at twelve weeks. I got it before leaving for deployment. I listen to it every night before going to sleep. All the things I claimed I would not allow myself to relive—that seems not to be working for me so far.

Baby girl, when you're old enough to understand and read this portion, just know I am sorry for not being there. I am so sorry! But I also want to say I'm sorry in advance for not being there in the future. Many years ago, when your daddy used to dream about a perfect life, a house, a car, kids, and to be married happily ever after, I never understood why it was so hard for the older people I used to watch growing up to get it right. I never understood how parents couldn't be there to watch their children's first steps, hear their first words, pick them up from school every single day, pack a nice lunch to take to school with the sandwich crust cut off, be there to see them off to prom and make their graduation. The idea of even missing you poop in the toilet for the first time made me cringe, and I knew I would do fatherhood differently. I had these grand plans of being a daddy to you before you were even thought of, but I find it harder than I thought. Sounds crazy, I know. *Just be there! It's not that hard!*

One day, Aubrey, you will see that there is a distinct difference between what you want out of life and what just happens to you. I planned to bring so much change, be so different, just to grow older and truly learn and understand that sometimes I just can't.

My tears hit the page as I wrote this part.

Some parts of me regret bringing you into this world. As a father, one of my jobs is to protect you from anything that can hurt you. If you love someone, you keep them from all the possible bad things, right? Well, baby girl, I brought you right into it. This world is so fucked up and twisted. I brought you into a place where you're gonna cry, a place where you're going to experience heartbreak and pain, a place where you're gonna get pushed down a lot and sometimes there is nothing you can do about it, baby. Why? Well you'll hear this phrase a lot—*it's just life.* The part that hurts me the most is realizing I can't be there with you every step of the way. I can't be there to wipe those tears every time. I can't be there to put that broken heart back together and rub your head for the pain. God, I can't be there to have my hand out before you get knocked down. You may question your existence. You may ask why sometimes. It's going to be hard, Aubrey, but here is what I need you to understand. People with the loudest boos usually have the cheapest seats and have the least support on the moves you make. So when those boos happen, because they will, you look up at the stands and then realize where you are: they came to watch you. Some people will tell you to never look back, ever. Well, baby girl, it's OK to look back sometimes. It will remind you why you started running in the first place. It may also remind you why you never want to look back. You are going to be the change this world needs to see. You are a muthafuckin' prodigy, the daughter of a king, so it's only right you keep your head up so that tiara doesn't slip off.

Just know, baby girl, everything I have done, everything I am doing, every word written in this book goes without saying. Understand that I love you to Pluto and back and there again. I can't wait to hold you in my arms for the first time because I know you look just like me. You're welcome for the genes. Baby girl, you can really do anything and accomplish *anything* if you put the work in.

In the same breath, I guess that was the whole motivation in writing this memoir. To show each and every one of you just that. Being a hard worker doesn't mean you only work hard at one thing. You have to have balance, authenticity, the *can't-be-stopped* mentality, and the desire mixed with a little finesse. Work hard at every goal, every aspect, and every facet in life because you never know what could happen.

All I am saying is anyone can be somebody, but it's up to you to decide what you will be. How does this story end? Well, that's the beauty of it all: it is still being written every day. Now there is only one question left to answer, and that is "Where do you go from here?"

Much love,

Signed Torrey Carnell Butler

ACKNOWLEDGEMENTS

I cannot express my gratitude enough for the profound people I have encountered in my life. Each and everyone of you has had a tremendous impact, that I will forever be grateful for.

Brandi Butler and Aubrey Butler, my beautiful family. Thank you for your continuous love and support through this process. Brandi you pushed me to not give up on this dream. You have supported me from the start, and I can't thank you enough. Aubrey you gave me the motivation to finish the journey. Always remember anything is possible. Thank you family!

Dianne Butler-Moore and Tiffanie Moore, words do not give justice to how much you have inspired me. Dianne, mama thank you for raising me to be the strong man I am today, I wouldn't be here without you both. Thank you!

Cochran Family, special shoutout to Edward Sr., Edward Jr., Eron and Michelle Cochran. Since we moved to Atlanta, GA., your family welcomed mines with open arms and I thank you. Thank you for being apart of my family.

Mr. Thaxter Kelley, this best mentor I could ask for. You have no idea how much you've molded me from our conversations. It didn't seem like it at the time, but I was listening. I heard you and I thank you!

Savannah State University, my alma mater. Thank you for giving me a chance at higher education. Also Captain Clark Price, I would be remised if I didn't say thank you. You gave me a shot. You allowed me to grow and develop as a man and leader in NROTC and I thank you.

Stockbridge High School NJROTC, Lenwood Stackhouse, Marvin Russell, Ralph Malone. If it weren't for you three giving me the guidance I needed and seeing something in me that I didn't see in myself, I wouldn't have made it this far. Thank you!

Tchanavia Lastie, you did amazing work with my photos. You have vision and you saw what I pictured in my head and brought it to life for this project. Check out her Instagram @ blackqueenphotography for great photography work.

Kevin Ijeh, dope videographer. You helped bring my notepad vision to motion. Thank you for your great vision and creativity. Check out his Instagram @kevin.creates for great videography work.

Robert Moore, even though you're not here physically I know you smile at my accomplishments. Thank you for taking on the demanding task by taking me in as your own child. You are forever loved and forever missed. Thank you!

I want to thank all my family and friends for your support. Shoutout to my Nassau, Bahamas family, I love you guys!

I especially want to acknowledge all the young girls and boys reading this. This book is for you, never give up on a dream because someone else thinks its silly or its been done before. The world is waiting on you. Show them something.